WITHDRAWN FROM STOCK

LUCAN LIBRARY
TO RENEW ANY ITEM TEL:

Items should be returned on or before the last date below. Fines, as displayed in the Library, will be charged on overdue items.

Renewing the Irish Church

Towards an Irish Liberation Theology

Joe McVeigh

Mercier Press

Mercier Press
PO Box 5, 5 French Church Street, Cork.
24 Lower Abbey Street, Dublin 1.

© 1993 Joe McVeigh

ISBN 1 85635 039 8

A CIP record for this book is available from the British Library

Dedicated to the memory of my Mother

Printed in Ireland by Colour Books.

Contents

Preface

There are at least two important experiences which influenced me in the writing of this book. The first is my experience of the progressive Church in the USA from 1980-1983. There I came in contact with people, in the Catholic Church and in other Christian communities, who were deeply committed to the cause of human rights and justice in many countries – people like the late Sister Marjorie Tuite who worked on Central America; Renny Golden and others like Peggy Billings at the NCC; people like Carolyn Forche who was speaking and writing about human rights abuses in many countries including Ireland; and Noel Correa who worked in a Nicaragua support group; people involved in the Catholic Worker movement, the Berrigans – Phil and Dan; Liz McAllister and their comrades who struggled for justice and human rights at home and abroad and, of course, the many committed people of all different backgrounds who worked for human rights and justice in Ireland. This was during the traumatic time of the hunger-strikes. The names of Bobby Sands and his comrades who sacrificed their lives for their deeply held principles were on the front pages almost daily in 1981. A support group, the H-Block/Armagh group, with which I was associated worked out of a Methodist Church in Washington Square, Manhattan. This time in the United States opened my eyes to the model of the Church which I had not seen in action before – the Church committed enthusiastically to the oppressed and to working for justice.

A second experience which helped to crystalise some of the ideas in this book took place in 1986 when I returned to Ireland. The priests of our diocese of Clogher along with our bishop held a week-long Assembly to discuss the role and ministry of the priest. While many useful issues were discussed, I was disappointed that the issue of injustice and discrimination which has led to the ongoing conflict in the north was not on the agenda. I felt then, and even more so now having read the published statements of the Hierarchy, the National Council of Priests and the Irish Commission for Justice and Peace (ICJP), that the Irish Church was avoiding a central issue affecting the lives of the people of this island.

The ideas in this book have also been influenced by my contact with priests and religious friends who work in Latin America, Asia and Africa and who have shared their experiences of Church with me. I am influenced by the writings and reflections of many Liberation theology writers. These and my own experience of working with various justice groups here have all helped to shape my views about the Church and my conviction about the need for radical renewal in the Irish Church if it is to become a Church that works for justice as well as being a voice for the voiceless.

I have benefited greatly from discussing these ideas with many people. I am deeply grateful to all who have helped in the preparation of this book, to Brian McDonald, Máire Ní Siocháin and Ann Gaughan; to Mary Feehan of Mercier Press for her encouragement and to Maria O'Donovan for her patience with the typing. Go raibh céad míle maith agaibh go léir. Beir Bua.

Seosamh Mac an Bheatha (Joe McVeigh)

Introduction

We belong to the category of nations that have been colonised, as distinct from those which have not or which themselves have been colonisers. And our reaction to this ravaging experience? We reacted somewhat, during the first half of this century, but it was only a half-hearted reaction ... So our present situation is that of a severely colonised nation which has not yet overcome the psychological and behavioural effects of colonisation ... (Desmond Fennell, 'A Theology for the Irish', Doctrine and Life, May 1977).

Ireland is a country of 'haves' and 'have nots'. The rich get richer and the poor get poorer because the economic system favours those who have money and property. This is true of both states, the 26 county state which has had a degree of independence since 1922 and the 6 county state which is still ruled by the Westminster parliament against the wishes of the majority of the Irish people. It is in the context of the striking inequality within this partitioned island that I examine the role of the Catholic Church – the Church in which the majority of the population has been baptised and educated and a Church which has had a powerful political influence in the life of this country.

This hierarchical Church is becoming increasingly irrelevant to many who are now disillusioned with its role in society as a supporter of a status quo which favours the rich against the poor. I show the potential for the growth of a new Church and a new homespun theology taking what is worthwhile from our own culture and traditions – in particular the notion of *meitheal* or local solidarity. I believe that there is potential for the growth of such a Church among the grassroots wherever small groups are active in social and justice issues. The development of such a grassroots Church could do a lot to counter the slave mentality (evident in a lot of community development and peace groups) as well as the low self-esteem and the dullness associated with religion and religious celebrations that still exists in this country.

Within the Catholic Church, especially since the Second

9

communal
Labour

Vatican Council which took place thirty years ago, a division has emerged between those who believe in a hierarchical/ authoritarian Church and those who believe in a communi- tarian/humanitarian Church. There are those who confine the Church's role to making theoretical statements about poverty and human rights while engaging in collaboration with governments; there are others who adopt a totally different role of prophetic witness which is aimed at em- powering the poor while also engaging in constant criticism of the political powers. There are still some who believe that the Church's mission is purely spiritual and that the Church should be neutral with nothing to say to the world in which we live out our lives.

For those who favour the liberation model of Church there are two starting points. The first is the existence of widespread human suffering and misery – not caused by fate or nature, but by political decisions. There are people struggling to change this unjust situation. The second start- ing point is the Gospel which shows quite clearly that Jesus Christ saw his mission in terms of supporting and empow- ering the poor and the marginalised. That suggests that the disciples of Jesus and the community to which they belong should adopt his way and bring it on further in whatever situation people find themselves. They take their inspiration from their faith understood in terms of discipleship, commit- ment and action (love of neighbour). Christian faith is very specific about this commitment to social betterment.

This approach has brought many sharp rebukes from those who promote the institutional model and who see themselves charged with the responsibility of maintaining the status quo and upholding the authority of the Vatican. There have been a number of negative criticisms of liber- ation theology. Some liberation theologians and activists have been censored and punished by the Church authorities. All of this is to be expected from a Church which is not as sure of itself as it was for several generations and a Church heavily influenced by people with a pre-Second Vatican Council mentality.

This conflict of opinion has also touched the Irish

Church – mostly in the realm of personal morality. But it is seen also in the approach of some to the social and political issues that face this country. There has been for a long period now a division within the Irish Church with regard to the political future of this country and the British government's denial of the Irish people's right to national self-determination. Within Ireland a partitionist mentality has developed partly as a result of the Catholic Church's acceptance of partition and its willingness to deal with the social and economic issues north and south as if these were not related and as if partition had no bearing on these issues.

Liberation theology is usually associated with the Church in Latin America. It has, undoubtedly, given many people there and throughout the world a new framework in which to live their lives according to the Gospels. It was in the context of the total disillusionment with the official Church's policy of supporting the status quo that liberation theology had its origins in the 1960s and 1970s. Small groups of committed Christians – not just Catholics – organised to campaign for social justice and a better quality of life for themselves and their neighbours. They sought to confront the root causes of the poverty and injustice that exist in society.

An Irish liberation theology will reflect the experience of the Irish people as an oppressed and colonised nation which has not yet achieved full political and economic freedom and control over its own affairs. It will deal with the causes, not the symptoms of violence, poverty and inequality. The British government and its agents have been quick to accuse Irish priests of 'meddling in politics' whenever they support the people against those in power. However, priests and religious must always take their cue from the Bible and the oppressed people – not the government.

This book is a follow up to *A Wounded Church*, published in 1989. It is offered as a further contribution to an understanding of the radical social and political demands of the Christian faith for Irish Catholics. One of the great needs we have in the Irish Catholic Church is for real education – education which raises our awareness about poverty/oppres-

11

sion and their causes as well as the power that people have when they organise to overcome injustice.

The Catholic Church has rich resources but these are not readily available to those who want to bring about radical change in Irish society. Without those resources at their disposal people have to find other ways of learning, meeting and of experimenting to bring about social change. Liberation theology offers a focus and a framework in which people can meet and work together in small groups to explore new ways of expressing their Christian faith.

The image or idea of the *meitheal* comes to mind when neighbour joined with neighbour to save the crops. An Irish liberation theology could become a *meitheal* theology since it is a theology of the people. Christianity has been and still is an important component of Irish culture. In the past religion and religious differences have been used by those in power to defend and uphold the political establishment irrespective of the injustice and undemocratic nature of that political system. It is now time that the people recovered their power. Liberation theology offers the people the opportunity to put social justice and social sin on the Church's agenda.

In this book, I argue for a new model of Church – a Church of the Poor and a Church for Liberation. The Church of the Poor is a Church of equals committed to equality in society. The present model of Church which has developed in Ireland over the past 200 years is a middle class, hierarchical and authoritarian organisation which is afraid of liberation and people power. This model of Church has failed everywhere else in the world to provide the people with an adequate vision for the future and an effective strategy for overcoming systematic injustice and institutional violence.

Only a radical change involving a new pastoral direction for the Irish Catholic Church can result in the Church here becoming the voice of the voiceless and confronting the root causes of poverty and inequality in this country.

1

Good News for Whom?

The whole Bible has been produced by the poor or from the perspective of the poor which permits them and only them to find the key to its interpretation ... (Pablo Richard, 'The Bible, the Historical Memory of the Poor', in *Lucha/Struggle*, 1985)

The chief subject of the study in the monastic schools of early Christian Ireland was the Bible. With the exception of such instruction as was of practical necessity for carrying on the services of the Church, all other studies, including that of the Fathers of the Church, were ancillary to the reading, comprehension and exposition of the scriptures. The predominance thereof is witnessed to by the whole literary remains of the early Irish Church (James Kenny, 'The Sources for the Early History of Ireland', in *Irish Spirituality*).

The proclamation of the Reign of Heaven is the most radical political and theological statement that could ever be made. It has nothing to do with being perfect. It has to do with basing our life on the Real. And for all of us that means we have to change our lives ... The Gospel is before all else a call to live differently, so that life can be shared with others. (Richard Rohr, *Simplicity*).

According to traditional Catholic theology and preaching Jesus is not someone who challenges unjust political and economic structures. The political implications of Jesus' life are hardly ever referred to or mentioned. That approach would most likely disturb and annoy a great many people who would protest that Jesus had nothing to say about politics. As for understanding Jesus as a radical or revolutionary with an important message for the poor and oppressed – that would be considered as heresy.

Yet Jesus said: 'Do you suppose that I am here to bring peace on earth? ... No, I tell you, but rather dissension. For from now on a household will be divided: three against two, and two against three: the father divided against the son, son against father, mother against daughter, daughter against mother: mother-in-law against daughter-in-law, daughter-in-law against mother-in-law' (Lk. 12: 51-53; Mt. 10: 34-36).

Jesus did bring dissension because his uncompromising political stance inevitably divided the people into those who were for and those who were against him.[1]

The question about the political implications of Jesus' mission is very relevant and very important for the Irish Church. It is a subject which has been studiously avoided in the teaching and preaching about Jesus because its implications have serious repercussions for the pro-establishment line adopted by the Catholic hierarchy. Jesus has been presented as someone who is 'above politics'. Such a caricature is entirely false and misleading.

How is it that there are so many different interpretations of what the Bible says? How can God's word be so blatantly misused to justify oppression and injustice? It has been used to justify colonialism and conquest. It is used by right-wing fundamentalists to intimidate people into accepting a very dogmatic and simplistic view of life. There is an old and true saying that 'the devil can quote scripture for his own purposes'.

The essential meaning of the Bible is that it is God's word on the poor in history – yesterday, today and in the future. The word of God in the Bible has been taken over and interpreted by those with a vested interest in maintaining the status quo. They recognised the power of this collection of writings and the esteem in which ordinary people hold it.

The problem with understanding the Bible is that it has been interpreted and preached by those who see the world only from the perspective of the 'respectable' people in society, those who support the status quo. It is they who have formed the predominant Catholic theology in Europe – quoting Scripture to suit themselves. That theology is rooted in a deep separation of religion and life. The Scriptures are preached in a way that avoids the political and religious implications of the message of Jesus and the prophets. They are taken out of their original context and are read in isolation – never as a unit.

In recent years the Bible has been reclaimed by the poor in many countries. It must always be remembered that it was composed by people who were constantly oppressed, by people with a holistic approach to life. For them there was no split between the sacred and the secular, religion and life. They were struggling for survival as a small nation, surrounded by much larger and more powerful countries. The Bible includes some of that history, some of their songs and prayers and some statements of their leaders on behalf of the poor and oppressed.

In order to rediscover the radical meaning of the Bible it is necessary to re-read it through the eyes of the poor and oppressed – since it was written by them and for them. Central to any understanding of the radical political implications of our faith is our understanding of the God of the Bible and the person of Jesus, his life, death and Resurrection.

Who is the God of the Bible? Some will say that this question is superfluous – that everyone knows that the God of the Bible 'is the one perfect being, all-powerful and all-wise, creator of heaven and earth, whose goodness and justice never fail' – or some similar definition. The suggestion is that all who say they believe in God are working with the same basic understanding. But the supposed common understanding of God in our western culture is deceptive. The long history of conflict between Christians in Latin America has shown that the common confession of one God hides different, and even opposing, ways of envisaging God. We can say in summary that the God of the Bible is the God who led Israel out of Egypt and who raised Jesus Christ from the dead.

The God of the Bible is a God who is found in the struggles of the poor and oppressed for justice and freedom. This is a God who demands justice – not the philosophical God of the academics nor the up-in-the-air God of the charismatics. The poor proclaim a God who liberates and gives life. Their experience of violent death and suffering leads to the affirmation of the God of Life.[2]

The God of the Bible is the God who acts in very specific and radical ways in history:

> The Lord feeds the hungry and sets prisoners free.
> The Lord loves the righteous and watches over the stranger.
> The Lord gives heart to the orphan and the widow
> (Ps 146: 5-9).

Some will argue that God who is good and loving must love everyone. But in the Bible the concrete expression of this love favoured the slaves in Egypt and Palestine and the poor of Galilee.

The God of the Bible is first and foremost the God who defends the poor and is accepted as such by the poor and oppressed. Yahweh/God is looked upon as the permanent defender of the poor whom Yahweh delivers from oppression:

> He delivers the needy who call on him,
> the afflicted with no one to help them.
> His mercy is upon the weak and the poor,
> to whom he is a protector.
> He rescues them from oppression and strife
> for their life is precious to him (Ps. 72:12-13).

The God of the Bible is the God of Life who defends the poor and oppressed. Those who are responsible for oppression and poverty do not believe in the same God; they believe in another God, an idol. This is seen most clearly in the greatest story of the Old Testament – the Exodus story – in which the name given to God is Yahweh:

> Yahweh spoke further to Moses, 'Thus shall you say to the Israelites: "the Lord (Yahweh), the God of your Fathers, the God of Abraham, the God of Isaac, the God of Jacob has sent me to you ... This is my name forever, this is my title for all generations"' (Ex. 3:13-15).

It was this Yahweh/God of the Exodus that the faithful Jews always revered and remembered. Whenever they turned away from that Liberator God they were called to repentance and conversion by their prophets and leaders.

> I, the Lord, am your God, who brought you out of the land of Egypt, the place of slavery. You shall not have other gods besides me. You shall not carve idols for yourselves in the image of anything in the sky above or on the earth below or in the waters beneath the earth; you shall not bow down before them or worship them. For I, the Lord your God, am a jealous God (Ex. 20: 2-5).

Even amongst the Jews – God's chosen people – history records that there were those who replaced the true God for an idol whenever they divorced their religious practice from the social and economic life of the community. Whenever the religious ruling class and business class continued to profess faith in Yahweh/God while engaging in the exploitation of the poor, the prophets spoke out:

> Woe to those who enact unjust laws
> And issue oppressive decrees!
> Woe to those who rob the poor of their rights
> And deprive my people of justice!
> They prey on grieving housewives and widows
> They terrorise the orphans and the helpless (Is. 10:1-2).

These people are reminded who God is and they are called to conversion or to stand condemned:

> Thus says the Lord, Israel's King
> and Redeemer, the Lord of hosts;
> I am the first and the last;
> there is no God but me ...
> Thus says the Lord your Redeemer,
> who formed you from the womb;
> I am the one who made all things,
> who alone stretched out the heavens;
> when I spread out the earth, who was with me? (Is. 44:6, 24).

The prophet, speaking for Yahweh/God, makes clear the kind of worship that is required if it is to be genuine:

> This rather, is the fasting that I wish:
> releasing those bound unjustly,

untying the thongs of the yoke;
Setting free the oppressed,
breaking every yoke,
Sharing your bread with the hungry,
sheltering the oppressed and the homeless;
Clothing the naked when you see them,
and not turning your back on your own (Is. 58: 6-7).

For the prophet, Amos, the great sinners were the swindling traders, who:

by lowering the bushel,
raising the shekel,
by swindling and tampering with the scales ...
can buy up the poor for money,
and the needy for a pair of sandals (Amos 8:5-6).

In the harsh warning to King Jehoiakim, the prophet Jeremiah contrasts the King's behaviour with that of his father who:

dispensed justice to the weak and the poor.
But your eyes and heart are set on nothing except your own
gain, or shedding innocent blood,
or practising oppression and extortion (Jer. 22: 16-17).

The yearning for power and wealth stops at nothing; it tramples underfoot the rights of others and disregards the commandments of the God who calls for the protection of the poor and oppressed. This self-seeking causes the powerful among the Jewish people to shed innocent blood and turn Israel into 'a city of blood' (Ex. 22:2) on which the Lord will pass judgment:

Her nobles within her are like wolves that tear prey, shedding blood and destroying lives to get unjust gain ... the people of the land practise extortion and robbery; they afflict the poor and the needy, and oppress the resident alien without justice (Ex. 22: 27, 29).

Oppression of the poor is here called by its real name – murder. God turned into an idol requires the shedding of blood. The author of the *Book of Sirach* says as much in striking language:

> Tainted his gifts who offers in sacrifice ill-gotten goods!
> Mock presents from the lawless win not God's favour.
> The Most High approves not the gifts of the Godless,
> nor for their many sacrifices does he forgive their sins.
> Like the man who slays a son in his father's presence is he who
> offers sacrifice from the possessions of the poor
> the bread of charity is life itself for the needy;
> he who withholds it is a man of blood.
> He slays his neighbour who deprives him of his living;
> he sheds blood who denies the labourer his wages (Sir. 34: 18-22).

The prophet Isaiah speaks of God's scorn for some of Israel's most esteemed institutions – the worship and the fast – because these practices were carried out by those who supported injustice. Isaiah addressed a situation where an arrogant upper-class exploited the poor. They were Churchgoing people who did not notice the suffering and impoverishment of the many;

> The Lord opens the indictment against the elders of his people
> and their officers. 'Those who have looked out for the poor,
> have ravaged the vineyard,
> and the spoils of the poor are in your houses.
> Is it nothing to you that you crush my people
> and grind the faces of the poor?' (Is. 3: 14-15).

The prophet Amos, a shepherd, was very angry at the way the poor were treated in the country. He condemned the rich for their behaviour:

> For crime after crime of Israel
> I will grant no reprieve,
> because they sell the innocent for silver
> and the destitute for a pair of shoes.
> They grind the heads of the poor into the earth
> and thrust the humble out of the way (Amos 2: 6-7).
>
> I will break down both winter-house and summer-house;
> houses of ivory shall perish,
> and great houses be demolished,
> This is the word of the Lord.

19

You cows of Bashan who live on the hills of Samaria,
you who oppress the poor and crush the destitute,
your time is coming
when they will carry you away on their shields (Amos 3; 15-
4:1).

The prophet Jeremiah adds his voice to the chorus of complaints:

Among the people there are wicked people,
who set death traps to catch others.
Their houses are full of fraud,
as a cage is full of birds,
they grow rich and grand,
bloated and rancorous;
their thoughts are all of evil,
and they refuse to do justice;
the claim of the orphan they do not put right,
nor do they grant justice to the poor (Jer. 5: 26-28).

The Old Testament ends on this pessimistic note. A people whose history began with their own liberation from injustice had themselves become the oppressors of the poor. Only a remnant remains to carry on the hope for justice – a hope which is embodied in the Messiah-king.

St Luke takes up the story. He speaks of a Messiah who has come to bring good news to the poor. The Gospel is good news, not for the rich, but for the poor:

The Spirit of the Lord is upon me,
He sent me to bring good news to the poor ... (Lk. 4: 18).

His ministry was inextricably linked to his faith in the reign of God. The Yahweh/God of the Bible, who sent his son, Jesus, into the world, is the God who has a plan in history in which he is inextricably bound through covenants.

The God of the Bible is inseparable from God's plan, God's kingdom. Every effort to find and understand God divorced from God's reign is, in the language of the Bible, an attempt to construct an idol. A God without a kingdom is a community or fetish, a work of our hands, a denial of the Lord, because such a separation is contrary to God's plan.

20

We know from the *Book of Genesis* that humans are created in the image of God – and are made for community, are meant to be equal. Because the love of God is so intense, there is a community of persons. That love is not even confined to the community of persons but extends to all creation. Human society ought to be modelled on the Trinity. There should be no class distinction.

The compassion of God is shown in the love for the oppressed and the poor and in the outrage at the oppression of the weak by the rich and powerful. It was demonstrated on many occasions throughout the history of the Israelite people – above all remembered in the Exodus event when the Jews were set free from slavery in Egypt and led by Moses to the Promised Land.

The God of the Exodus sent his son to live with the people he had chosen. This God became flesh and identified with humanity for all time and in every place. This God identified with the poorest, the most marginalised. The God of the Bible, by the time of the New Testament, is not just one person – but three – a Trinity of Father, Son and Holy Spirit – indicating community and offering a model of unity and community for the whole human family.

Jesus took on the struggle of the poor and oppressed and he became a victim of the unjust political, economic and religious system that had been built by those whose only interest was personal power and the accumulation of riches. Jesus took on the struggle against this selfishness and greed and the unjust structures that protect this. He was killed – but he was raised from the tomb – another way of saying 'you cannot kill the truth – even if you think you can'. The Resurrection has many political implications.

After he was crucified some of his disciples came to believe that he was still alive in a new way – prompting them and encouraging them. They banded together to continue his ministry and preach his radical message. That was the origin of the Church. It was based on faith in the Resurrection of Jesus by which God confirmed Jesus and his values and showed that the system which caused death and suffering for so many could be beaten. In the Resurrection,

God the Father affirms the ministry of Jesus who stood with the poor and who suffered the fate of all those who challenge injustice.

To place the struggle for justice and equality in a religious context is a radical approach which leads to an inevitable conflict with the existing social and political order. However, it is the only way to bring about real change, ie, structural change, and to create a new society where people are to be treated justly and fairly as God intended.

This is the consequence of faith in the God of the Bible. That is why we state that faith has political implications which cannot be avoided without negating the Gospel. Those who advocate a religion which does not make radical political demands and without advocating the need for radical social and political change are those whom Jesus called 'hypocrites'. Those who profess belief in the Holy Spirit without recognising the need for that Spirit to reform the social and political systems are dishonest people according to Jesus.

There is freedom in many countries to preach the Gospel, to speak in tongues, to conduct healing ministries, and even to cast out evil spirits. Governments and Churches encourage religious movements like the charismatics, Cursillo and Search so long as they ignore the social and political realities of life around them, and remain emotional, individual and private.

The reality of the world we live in – where two-thirds of the people live in poverty and starvation while one-third have too much – is far removed from the vision of Jesus and the model of community life offered by the Trinity. It is the scandal of the division between rich and poor in society that the true believer in God has to be concerned about above all else. That is what the Christian community must be concerned about first and foremost. If it is not and is instead caught up in the promoting of its own image and seeking after power, status and wealth it is truly engaged in idolatry – the worship of false gods.

While the life of Jesus cannot be reduced to politics alone, it has serious political implications and can only be properly understood in the context of revolutionary politics. In that sense Jesus was a revolutionary. His idea of revolution is summed up in the phrase 'the kingdom of God'. It is in his proclamation that 'the kingdom of God is at hand' that we discover his radical politics and his relevance for today. He used imagination and power to deal with the corruption and abuse of human rights he saw happening all around him.

The idea of the 'kingdom' or 'reign of God' must be viewed in the context of the Bible as a whole and what it has to say about justice and freedom for the Jewish people. The message and mission of Jesus of Nazareth cannot be understood in isolation from the Old Testament Jewish tradition to which he belonged. In that tradition there is a great deal of emphasis on the need for justice if the Jewish people – God's chosen people – are to experience peace (shalom). Throughout the Old Testament God condemned injustice not in the abstract but in particular political and historical situations. The oppression of the Jews in Egypt was denounced. God intervened to rescue them and appointed a leader to lead them to freedom and to a new country. That liberation event is central in the history of the Jewish people. Already, before Christ, the prophets had often reminded the people that God was on the side of the poor and was opposed to the greed and corruption of the rich.

Jesus describes this work of changing political structures as building the 'kingdom' or reign of God. If you work for justice and freedom you are challenging the status quo – you are making the 'kingdom of God' happen. Jesus belongs to the tradition of the prophets; he announces his ministry and mission in terms similar to the great prophets – Jeremiah, Amos, Isaiah. Above all he shows what the kingdom of God means in the way he identifies with the poor and oppressed in his own country. He announced his vision of his ministry by quoting the words of Isaiah the prophet:

> He has sent me to bring the good news to the poor,
> to proclaim liberty to captives
> and to the blind new sight,

to set the downtrodden free,
to proclaim the Lord's year of favour ... The text is being
fulfilled today even as you listen (Lk. 4: 18-21).

Not only does Jesus see himself in the line of the Old Testament prophets but within the political mission of the prophets. The good news is first of all to the poor and to prisoners and what is announced is liberation. The good news is that poverty and oppression is not God's will for the poor; it is not the way God intended things to be and it must be changed. He introduces a definite note of hope into human affairs especially for the poor who were (and are) often resigned to their lot. Jesus was challenging the prevailing middle class theology and bias against the poor.

This text in Lk. 4 taken in conjunction with Matt. 25 shows clearly the political demands of Jesus' ministry and the political demands of the mission of those who would be his followers. In Matt. 25 Jesus declares quite plainly who it is that he identifies with and what he expects of his disciples:

The king will say to those on his right:
'Come, blessed of my Father! Take possession of the kingdom prepared for you from the beginning of the world. For I was hungry and you fed me, I was thirsty and you gave me drink. I was a stranger and you welcomed me into your house. I was naked and you clothed me. I was sick and you visited me. I was in prison and you went to see me' (Matt. 25: 34-36).

Jesus spells out in a very concrete way, how he expects his followers to act; to answer the needs of the hungry, thirsty, the homeless, those in need of clothing, those who are ill, those in prison. Activity with regard to those in need is identified with activity towards the Son of Man. These words of Jesus spell out a political mission for the Church. These are material, and, therefore, political concerns. They cannot be shirked or neglected without denying Christ himself. By taking these concerns on board we in the Church are immediately entering the political arena.

All of this is understood within the context of 'the kingdom or reign of God' which Jesus proclaimed at the beginning of his ministry: 'The Kingdom of God is close at hand.

Repent' (Mk 1: 15, Matt. 4:17). This was very important to him. It meant that there was a certain urgency about his message and his mission. The kingdom is a reality in the world now but it is not yet fully realised. It is challenging people (the rich and those in power) and the Church to respond to his call to make an option for the poor and the oppressed. There can be no question of opting out or of making excuses.

What kind of political message had Jesus? His vision was of a new society without privilege rather than the existing society which he saw around him – a society which favours some and excludes or marginalises those who have no status. According to Jesus those who had no status were given status. 'Those first will be last and the last first.' Children were his model because they had no social status.

Jesus made a distinction between the peace that God wants and the peace that the world wants (Jn 14: 27). The peace that God wants is a peace that is based on truth, justice and love. The peace that the world – an imperfect world that adores idols – offers is a superficial peace that compromises the truth, that covers over the injustices and that is usually settled on for selfish purposes. 'There is no question of pre-serving peace and unity at all costs, even at the cost of truth and justice. Rather it is a matter of promoting truth and justice at all costs, even at the cost of creating conflict and dissension along the way.'[3] There can be no peace or recon-ciliation without justice and the recognition of peoples' basic rights. Those who use the Gospel selectively to preach a message of reconciliation without justice are being dis-honest.

When Jesus spoke about 'love' it was not something vague and romantic. It was something concrete and chal-lenging (cf. The Good Samaritan). Loving the neighbour meant working to end the injustice and the unjust structures which prevented people from living dignified lives. Jesus was not crucified because he preached some vague 'ser-mons' about loving God and your neighbour. In Palestine, crucifixion was the punishment reserved for political criminals and rebel slaves. There is no way of avoiding the fact that Jesus was executed as a rebel – a revolutionary who took the side of the oppressed in the Galilee of his day. That was why Pilate had fixed to his cross the inscription 'This is Jesus, the King of the Jews' (Matt. 27:37).

While in Galilee he had come into conflict with the religious authorities and later with the political authorities. According to Jesus, salvation was not confined to saving souls but to good acts of healing, sharing meals etc. God's salvation is seen in every good human act. The preoccupation with salvation meaning life after death is a complete distortion of what Jesus was about. It makes the poor easy to subjugate. For those higher up the social ladder they see it in terms of what is in it for me, that is, on a consumer basis. Personal salvation is all that matters. This distortion of the Bible's message leads to a turning away from the real God – to a turning away from the real needs of others.

Nor is the kingdom of God built simply by liturgical celebrations. The real work of building the kingdom is done in the political sphere. Only God can bring about the kingdom but we can be signs of that kingdom by the values we uphold and pursue – above all the values of truth, justice, courage and freedom. These are the values that determine God's will – not resignation, cowardice or apathy in the face of oppression.

To be a Christian in the world today means to live in the Spirit of Christ as we find that described in the Bible and as is kept alive in the historical memory of the poor. Faith in Christ calls for reverence for all of God's creation and openness to the Spirit of God who empowers people to work for a just society.

This faith is lived out and worked out in community with others. In a structured way it is lived out within Churches or sects. For most Catholics the faith is lived out within the Roman Catholic Church which has become through the centuries a highly structured organisation with its own rules and regulations. It has developed its own theology and political policy – a pragmatic and defensive approach to ensure its continued existence – often in hostile situations. The Church is a movement within history and is, therefore, part of history. However, it must always be renewing itself so that it does not become contaminated with the power struggles of this world.

The Church was intended from the beginning to be a missionary Church in the sense of a Church which brings good news and hope to the poor and oppressed in their historical struggle for justice and freedom. A look at the history of the Church shows us that often this role was turned on its head.

Within the Catholic Church – not to mention the other Christian Churches – there are many different understandings of what faith in Jesus means and demands. The Gospel has often been distorted – for political and pragmatic reasons – and instead of its being good news for the poor it often became very bad news for them and good news for the rich. The radical political demands of faith in the God of Jesus, the God of the Bible, has been totally distorted to equate obedience to the state with obedience to God.

Faith in the Spirit of God active in the people's struggle for justice has been ignored in practice. Liberation theology seeks to recover that sense of the Spirit working in the lives of the poor and oppressed, to bring about justice. Those engaged in liberation theology are seeking to create a totally new model of Church which confronts and challenges 'the powers and principalities' of this world as well as the paternalism and authoritarianism of the Church itself. In doing so they are witnessing to the presence of God's reign here and now.

2

Whose Side is the Church on?

*In the order of human society as established by God there are rulers
and ruled, employers and employees, rich and poor, learned and
ignorant, nobility and proletaria* (Pope Pius X 1903).

*We are invited to look at life from the viewpoint of the poor. That
means seeing it from where the Lord took his place in order to grant
us salvation. His life teaches us that this perspective is the most
generous, the most universal. This attitude leads us to listen
carefully to the cries of the suffering people, to support their
initiatives in solidarity, and to respect the organisations the people
set up to meet their basic needs* (Chilean Bishops: *Maryknoll
Magazine*, January 1986).

When Hitler was in power in Germany both the Vatican and
the German Catholic bishops remained silent about the
atrocities that were carried out by his regime. When there
was an attempt made to assassinate him in November 1939,
the bishops went a step further. Cardinal Bertram, in the
name of the German bishops, and Cardinal Faulhaber, in the
name of the Bavarian bishops, sent telegrams to the German
dictator expressing their support and solidarity. The bishops
urged their people to accept Hitler on the basis that his was
the duly constituted authority.

In a joint pastoral letter issued a few days after the
invasion of Catholic Poland, the Catholic bishops declared
that Hitler was waging a just war in the eyes of God:

> In this decisive hour we encourage and admonish our Catholic
> soldiers in obedience to the Fuhrer, to do their duty and to be
> ready to sacrifice their whole person. We appeal to the faithful
> to join in ardent prayers that God's providence may lead this
> war to blessed success and peace for fatherland and people.[1]

The bishops of the Catholic Church in the allied countries found that the war being waged by Hitler's opponents was also a just war. God, it would seem, was working for both sides.

It is instructive to read the official statements and pastorals of the Catholic Church. They reflect the official Church's understanding of its role with regard to the state and fascist governments. Official statements give us some idea of the various interpretations of the role of the Church in society at particular periods in history and in particular situations.

Two periods in modern history point up the Catholic Church's understanding of its role in society as the defender of the status quo. One is the period after the French Revolution (1789) and the other is that period which saw the rise of fascism after the First World War (1918-1939).

The official response of the Catholic Church to the French Revolution was determined by the Church's close alliance with the French monarchy. Also many senior clergy had been killed and Church buildings were destroyed. The Church authorities reacted bitterly to the revolution and to the idea of democracy or people-power. The Church, not being a democratic organisation itself, favoured the monarchical system of government and opposed Republicanism in France as in Ireland.

With regard to the rise of fascism in the 1930s the Catholic Church appears to have had no difficulty in accepting fascist governments. The official Catholic Church entered into agreements with the governments of Hitler, Mussolini and Franco and the Vichy government of Pétain in France. Such collusion raises serious questions about the influence of the Vatican in European politics on the side of those who promised 'strong government':

> Since subsidies to the Church and Catholic education of school children were provided for in these agreements it found that they (the fascist governments) observed 'good morals' ... After World War II the Vatican sought to mend its damaged prestige by establishing anti-fascist credentials. It pointed to members of the lower clergy who had participated in the Italian resis-

tance in the latter stages of the war and to Catholic priests who
had been victims of the Nazi regime. It also published documents showing frictions between the Holy See and Hitler's
government. But these frictions arose from conflicts over the
institutional power of the Church, not any concern for human
rights on the part of the Holy Father, and the priests who
bravely resisted the Nazis, did so against the adjurations of
their bishops. The record of collaboration between the Church
and both German and Italian fascism cannot be expunged.[2]

The rationale for the support of Hitler was the insistence on
obedience to duly-constituted authority. However, this
demand for obedience did not prevent the official Church
from giving its blessing to those who engaged in counter-
revolutions in Mexico and Spain where the official Church
was not in favour with the governments in power.

In more recent years we have witnessed Catholic
bishops give their blessing to the American army in Viet-
nam, the British army in the Falklands and the combined
US-led forces in the Gulf war. All of this raises serious questions about the political alliance of the official Church with
the western alliance – the North Atlantic Alliance – and its
attitude to structural injustice throughout the world which is
the result of economic policies pursued by the super-powers.
One wonders if the official Church is willing to read 'the
signs of the times' in relation to the foreign policies of the US
as it extends its influence throughout the world.

The Catholic Church, like the other Christian Churches,
claims to have its origins in the ministry and preaching of a
humble worker from Galilee, who lived at Nazareth about
2,000 years ago. Central to the original teaching of this
prophet is the concept that the Rule (Kingdom) of God is a
concept with radical political connotations. The proof of this
is that his ministry of healing and helping the poor and his
teaching which upset the establishment led to his crucifixion
on a cross – a penalty reserved by the Roman authorities for
what were considered political offences.

It must be remembered that the New Testament was
written when Palestine was occupied by the Romans. Given
this context the idea of the 'reign of God' had radical, indeed

revolutionary political implications. With its primary concern for justice for the poor it could be perceived as challenging the status quo which kept the mass of the people poor and marginalised. This is how a present-day writer and activist in the Philippines describes the uniqueness of Christ's message:

> The kingdom is not exclusively spiritual and other-worldly but embraces all of human life – economic, social, political, cultural and religious dimensions – and is to begin to become visible in this world. The early Christian community certainly understood it in this way. They were not satisfied with liturgical unity (worshipping together).[3]

After only a few centuries as a missionary movement, forming small communities committed to liberation, and within a few years of establishing a community in Rome where Christians were perceived as threats to the established power, Christianity was adopted as the state religion of the Roman Empire. As a result of this alliance of the Chrisitan religion with the Empire, the radical nature of Jesus Christ's teaching about 'the Reign of God' became completely distorted and indeed, suppressed. It came to be misinterpreted – most commonly in terms of another heavenly world after this life. There was a separation of the spiritual and the temporal, the sacred and the secular, a separation that has affected the way most Christians think about religion and life to this day. Mainly, as a result of the influence of Greek and Roman philosophy on the Christian message the essentially radical and holistic approach of Jesus and the first apostles was suppressed.

That separation of faith and morality, religion and life, has had devastating results for the poor and for indigenous peoples in many countries. The political implications of the kingdom or reign of God were suppressed as the Church became part of the political establishment and became allied with Empires and rulers who massacred millions of people in their pursuit of power and wealth. This dualism which had already become part of Christian thinking by the Middle Ages meant that you could, at the same time, save souls and punish bodies.

As the Church grew in political power and influence its own understanding of its role could be summarised: to save souls, to inculcate obedience to the temporal authorities and to preserve the status quo – especially the monarchy. The official Catholic Church became arrogant and autocratic. It was vehemently opposed to change, to democracy, to women's rights and equality, to freedom of speech; in fact, to all progressive movements.

At the official level, the preaching of the Gospel lost its original emphasis on the presence of the Holy Spirit working creatively in communities to renew and transform all aspects of life – including the political and economic structures. Until the Second Vatican Council there was little talk of the need for social justice in the context of faith and salvation. As preached by the official Church, the Gospel came to legitimise the status quo. Instead of being Good News for the poor, it became good news for the rich and powerful. The poor were often reminded that their condition was 'the will of God' and that if they did not enjoy much happiness or prosperity in this life they most certainly would make up for it in the next. This interpretation of Christianity is still prevalent in many places.

In contrast to this distorted view of the Christian religion, the first Christian disciples – a small band of relatively poor people from the Galilee area of Palestine – were convinced that the new 'religion' of Jesus had important social/ political implications. His crucifixion, as a subversive and his resurrection, confirmed their belief. They believed that God had vindicated Jesus and his option for the poor and oppressed by raising him from the dead. It was their conviction about the power of Jesus and his vision that held them together and motivated them to carry on the mission begun by Jesus. Their faith in the power of God working now through the Holy Spirit in their small community to bring about change gave them courage to go out to the towns and villages spreading the good news – raising consciousness among the ordinary working people. These early disciples of Jesus belonged to a movement – rather than to a

Church, as we know it.

It was more than 200 years after the apostles that the Christians formed what became known as 'the Church' or 'assembly of believers'. Since then this 'assembly of believers' has fragmented. Different Christian Churches have developed their own structures, rules and traditions which have often become a source of division rather than unity and creativity. The different Churches became caught up in their own self-expansion and self-preservation as they lost sight of their original purpose.

Since the Second Vatican Council (1961-65) and the Medellin Council in 1968, small Christian communities in many countries are rediscovering the authentic Christian message through a rereading of the Scriptures and writings of the Early Church theologians. Their focus is the teaching of Jesus about the 'kingdom of God' – a kingdom of justice and truth. They are rediscovering the power of the Spirit at work where the poor and oppressed are struggling for freedom and justice. That is to say they are rediscovering the political implications of the New and Old Testaments through reflecting on their own situation of injustice and the marginalisation of the poor no matter what the risks involved in terms of persecution and loss of status. One such community in Soltentiname, Nicaragua has left us a unique collection of its thoughts and insights into the Gospel.[4]

The Early Church Fathers – those who wrote explaining and proclaiming the message of Jesus to the new communities of believers in the Middle East, North Africa and throughout Europe – have provided us with a valuable collection of writings which give an insight into how the early Church understood the message of Christ. They pay special attention to social justice as an issue of central importance and concern to the new Christian community. One of these, John Chrysostom, Bishop of Constantinople, writing about wealth and poverty around the year 400 AD asked:

> Tell me then how did you become so rich? From whom did you receive that large estate and from whom did he receive it who transmitted it to you? ... The root and origin of it must

have been injustice. Why? Because God in the beginning did not make one man rich and another poor ... He left the earth free to all alike. Why then if it is common have you so many acres of land while your neighbour has none? Is this not evil that you alone enjoy what is common to all?[5]

John Chrysostom was not popular with the large land-owners but he continued to denounce them:

This is robbery – not to share ones resources. Perhaps what I am saying astonishes you. Not only to rob others' property but also not to share your own with others is robbery and greed and theft ... The rich are in possession of the property of the poor even if it is patrimony they have received, even if they have gathered their money elsewhere.[6]

Ambrose, a bishop in Milan also refers to the causes of poverty:

Do spacious halls exalt you? They should rather sting you with remorse, because while they hold crowds they exclude the cry of the poor ... The naked man cries before your house and you neglect him. He cries, and you are solicitous as to what marble you will use to cover your floor.[7]

The Early Christian Fathers also saw the relationship between the Eucharistic celebration and concern for the poor. John Chrysostom declared:

Do not honour Christ here in Church clothed in silk vestments and then pass him by unclothed and frozen outside ... God does not heed golden vessels but golden hearts.[8]

Augustine stressed that all property should be held in common:

You have a common universe with the rich ... You do have a common sky, a common light ... have you brought along anything here? No, not even you rich people have brought anything. You have found everything here. With the poor you were born naked.

And elsewhere Augustine wrote:

God gives the world to the poor as well as to the rich ... Those who offer something to the poor should not think that they are doing so from what is their own.[9]

The modern reader is struck by the directness of these statements of the early Church writers:

Legality is not the question. Justice is the question. The early Christian moral philosophers held that there could be no justice in the matter of private property unless the expropriating rich were to restore to the poor the common goods which they had stolen from them.[10]

The situation of the Christian community changed in the fourth century. Instead of being marginalised and persecuted, Christianity was now tolerated, according to the Edict of Milan (313 AD), and quickly became the religion of the Roman state and empire, according to the Decree of Thessolonica (381 AD).

The proclamation of the Gospel message was then protected by the support of political authority and the Christianisation of the world of that time received a powerful impulse. The rapid advance of Christianity brought about a change in the manner of conceiving the relationship of mankind to salvation. It began to be thought that there were only two kinds of people; those who have accepted faith in Christ and those who have culpably rejected it ... the Church was regarded as the sole repository of religious truth. In a spontaneous and inevitable fashion there arose an ecclesiocentric perspective which centred more and more on the life of the Church – and continues to do so even up to the present time.[11]

As a result of this shift of perspective, the Catholic Church hierarchy often failed to address the issue of social injustice. There was not much tolerance of those who were not baptised members of the Church. There was not a great deal of respect for women in the Church. This is reflected in much of the theology that developed after Thomas Aquinas. It is still evident in many of the official Church pronouncements – and their attitudes to issues directly relating to women, marriage and the family.

The Catholic Church, in common with the other Christian Churches, has a tradition of teaching and practising concern for the poor – but this 'concern' has expressed itself in different forms down through the years. At times it did not figure in the official teaching and preaching or on the Church's agenda. It was not high on the official agenda when the Catholic Church became caught up in political intrigues and colonial expansion of the European empires throughout the sixteenth and seventeenth centuries. From then onwards the aim of a very institutional, authoritarian and hierarchical Church seems to have been social control rather than social justice.

The official Catholic Church (at the level of the Vatican and the various national episcopal conferences) did not want to give up the power and control that it had acquired. It was involved in treaties and concordats in return for power and financial support. This compromised its position as a prophetic voice in society. The Concordats in Italy in 1929 and Germany in 1933 effectively tied the Catholic Church to these two fascist states – with the result that it was not as vocal as it should have been in denouncing these tyrannies. The Catholic Church did not condemn the genocide of the Jews. The Pope was not prepared to jeopardise the privileged status won for the Church.

When fascism was defeated in these countries – but not in Spain – the Church made a new arrangement with the new right-wing Christian Democrat governments. These political alliances occurred while the Church proclaimed a social message about human rights and the subordination of the right to private property to the needs of all. Their actions were clearly in contradiction to their words. The official Church had become so obsessed with the dangers of socialism that the human rights dimension of the Church's teaching was played down. It was only with Pope John XXIII (1958-1965) that a change occurred and the emphasis on social justice was restored.

However, throughout the history of Christianity, there have been individuals and organisations who by the heroic witness of their lives have challenged the Churches to return to their roots in the Gospel. We can think of people like St Vincent de Paul (1581-1660) and St Francis of Assisi (1181-1226), Bartolme de Las Casas (1474-1566)[12], St Catherine of Sienna (died 1380), Dietrich Bonhoeffer (died 1945) and Pope John XXIII (died 1965).

For the Catholic Church, the Second Vatican Council (1961-65), called by Pope John XXIII, was a watershed. The renewed emphasis on the social teaching of the Church and on respect for human rights has motivated many Catholics to take up the cause of justice and liberation wherever oppressed people are struggling for their rights:

> Traditional Catholicism presented human life as a transitory phase on the way to 'heaven'; earthly life was essentially a kind of trial. Vatican II reversed that by stressing the continuity between earthly progress and ultimate transcendence.[13]

The Second Vatican Council marked a profound change in the Church's understanding of its role and purpose:

> Vatican II replaced the judicial, hierarchical definition of Church with more biblical and symbolic images ... in Latin America, where liberation theology sees Church not as institution but as movement in service to human liberation. The papal documents do not go this far, but they do express a new realisation of Church as servant to humanity in its struggle for peace, justice and development.[14]

After the Medellin conference of Latin American bishops in 1968, the 'preferential option of the poor' became, for a time at least, the official policy of the Latin American Church and encouraged the growth of liberation theology. It appeared that the Catholic Church had made a break with its past and entered on a completely new path:

> How do we explain the fact that the Church's 'preferential option for the poor' appears so new today? Such an option is not new: history shows that the option has always been, or at least tried to be, concerned with the poor. This has always been true, at least in intention, a principle never denied as such, so why does 'the option for the poor' seem like a new phenomenon today? It is because today it has taken on a new form,

that of a strategic option; it is now a matter of opting for the struggles of the poor, of working in solidarity with them, of associating with them as the protagonists of history. It is no longer a matter of bending over them full of mercy, like the Samaritan; it is now a political question: that of walking along the way of the oppressed ..."[15]

The option for the poor is new and different from anything that went immediately before because it meant the identification of the Church with the struggles of the poor and the end of colonialism. It is not simply about charity or helping the poor on an individual basis. It is about supporting democratic movements. It is about putting the poor in first place – in Church and in society. According to John XXIII in his radio message of 11 September 1962:

A Church of the poor is a Church in which the poor are privileged, a Church in which the poor occupy the first rank. This means that there is also room in it for the rich, but only to the extent that they are converted and fraternise with the humble. It is not true that the Church of the poor is against the rich; what it is against are the privileges, illegitimate interests and anti-evangelical pretensions of the rich. Therefore, the Church is and wishes itself to be the Church of all, but especially the Church of the poor.[16]

However, it would be wrong to think that the official Catholic Church policy towards poverty has radically changed. It is still very much one of charity rather than working for justice. While there have been progressive elements working for radical social change others in authority have adopted the terminology of liberation while opposing those who work for the fundamental restructuring of society. Pope John Paul II, while certainly expressing great concern about the poor, reveals in some statements, his belief in charity rather than justice:

Christ teaches us detachment from riches, trust in God and readiness to share. He urges us to look at our brothers and sisters who are poor and suffering from the point of view of one who – in poverty – knows what it is to be totally dependent on God and to stand in absolute need of him. The way we live will thus be the true and authentic measure of love of him

38

who is the source of life and love, as well as the sign of our faithfulness to the Gospel which he preached. May this Lenten season heighten this awareness in all of us and increase our *commitment to charity*.[17] (Italics added)

This traditional interpretation of the Church's mission in the world has been challenged by a more biblical understanding which sees the Church's mission in terms of a movement in solidarity with the poor in their struggle for justice rather than as an agent of charity and social control. There has been a redefinition of theology which is understood in terms of a commitment to liberation:

> A theology today which does not place at the centre of its concerns the poor, justice, freedom and liberation will have difficulty in refuting the accusation of alienation and even cynicism, and will in the end become totally irrelevant. The credibility of the Churches and of Christian thought is now being measured by the way in which they face the question of the poor.[18]

This new interpretation of the Gospels has brought warnings and condemnations from the Vatican where the Roman Curia has been leading a retreat from many of the advances which came in the wake of the Second Vatican Council. In many places throughout the world, including the US, progressive bishops have been harassed and replaced by conservative bishops. The case of Archbishop Hunthausen in Seattle is a typical example. At the behest of reactionary elements within the US Church, his progressive views resulted in his being censored and humiliated by the Vatican.[19]

Some liberation theologians and bishops have been censored and silenced. Leonardo Boff, one of the most prolific writers in the Liberation theology movement, has been forced out of the priesthood altogether. Many continue, however, in their pursuit of justice and in redefining the role of the Church in the world.

Above all they continue to proclaim the essential link between working for justice and the celebration of the Eucharist. If the Eucharist is to have real meaning or power then it must be linked to the work of social justice. Christians

39

who come together to celebrate the Eucharist are being challenged by the poor. For Catholics for whom the weekly celebration of the Mass may have become a routine ritual, there is need for a new understanding of the essential link between the weekly celebration of the Mass and working for social justice:

> The authentic celebration of the Eucharist requires some form of social action for justice by the community, directed towards the values of the kingdom of God. The Eucharistic community should be a force in the world for the transformation of society. Insofar as this liberating action is absent from the Mass, so to that extent we have to say that an essential element of the Eucharistic mystery is missing.[20]

The celebration of the Eucharist must lead people to take action for justice. It must sensitise people making them aware of the terrible poverty and oppression in their midst. It should create in people a sense of outrage and compassion:

> The hallmark of the new covenant ushered in by Jesus is compassion – this was the one foretold by Jeremiah: 'I will put my Law within them and I will write it upon their hearts; and I will be their God and they will be my people' (Jer. 31:33).[21]

Archbishop Romero, who was assassinated in 1980 by government agents, was a man of compassion; he was not afraid to speak out against the evil of injustice. He knew that it could be costly for the Church and for himself but he was not deterred. He was not content with private diplomatic representations but took a public stance against the corruption of the political and military authorities. Romero recognised that pity is not enough if there is to be a change. There is need also to work along with the people and to educate for social change. If the Good Samaritan were to travel along the road from Jerusalem to Jericho every day for a year and every day meet another victim, what does he do? Does he continue with his acts of charity or does he confront the reasons for this happening?

Charity alone is not effective in ending poverty and oppression. Helder Camara of Brazil writes about his conversion to the struggle of the poor and the work for justice:

At one time not only the Brazilian bishops but all the bishops of Latin America thought that our duty as shepherds was to uphold authority; we believed that without authority there would be chaos. We were to help maintain the existing social order. In that phase we were closely linked with the governments in power and with the rich. It is interesting (and I remember very well) that at that time no one accused me of meddling in politics. It seemed normal that Christ's Church was helping to maintain the governments and the rich in power ... But when the United Nations proclaimed that more than two-thirds of humanity lived in less than human conditions, we began to ask ourselves how we could continue being one of the main pillars of a social order that was, in fact, more than an established system of disorder. So without ever preaching hatred or violence, we endeavoured to denounce injustice and to promote a more dignified life for those mired in inhuman situations.[22]

There were two distinct phases:

During the first phase we worked for the people. But the Holy Spirit made us see the difference between working for the people and working with them. The difference seems small but it is really enormous. Today our major efforts go into showing that those beings living in less than human conditions – situations more animal-like than human – are God's children ... God is the father of all. He does not want to be father only to a small group of people and step-father to the rest of humanity. Christ said that he came so that all might have life and have it in abundance. And no one can tell us that he was referring only to spiritual matters, because when Christ comes to judge us he will say: I was hungry, thirsty, naked ... 'And woe to those who have not had eyes to see their brother or sister being trampled on and oppressed – the living Christ! Woe to those who refuse to be concerned about the situation of their fellow human beings, who fail to draw close to the oppressed ...'[23]

These words of warning from a modern prophet are a clear reminder that the Christian Church has a unique role in our world. That role is based on understanding the words of Jesus in terms of defending the poor and not the status quo.

41

We, as Christians, are invited, as the Chilean bishops recognised in their statement in 1985, to look at life and to read the scriptures from the viewpoint of the poor. That should make all the difference in the world as to how we understand our responsibilities as baptised members of the Church. That new awareness has led to the phenomenal growth of the liberation theology movement during the past two decades.

3

The Origins of Liberation Theology

Theology may be put at the service of oppression, death and destruction. For example there was a theology of slavery. The theologians of Salamanca with full seriousness at the time of the Spanish colonisation of Latin America, raised the question whether or not the Indians had souls!
(D Barbé, Grace and Power).

When the Second Vatican Council ended in 1965, Camillo Torres, a priest in Colombia, had already left the active ministry to join the Colombian revolutionary army. Earlier that year he held a press conference to inform the people why he had decided to leave the ministry and take up arms alongside the revolutionaries:

> I opted for Christianity because I felt it was there I would find the purest way of serving my neighbour. I was chosen by Christ to be a priest forever and motivated by the desire to give myself full-time to the love of my fellow human beings ... But when there are circumstances which prevent men and women from giving themselves to Christ, the function of the priest is to alter those circumstances, even though it may cost him the possibility of celebrating the Eucharist – a ritual that is not understandable unless it involves a total commitment on the part of Christians ... I have found it impossible to continue exercising my priesthood through the celebration of the liturgy within the present structure of the Church. However, the Christian priesthood is not just external or liturgical.[1]

Torres was deeply committed to bringing about justice in his native country. To bring that about there had to be revolutionary change in Colombia. He wanted a better quality of life for the long-suffering section of the population who were poor and powerless. He felt it necessary to join with the guerrilla army to resist those forces which upheld the unjust system of government. Torres had been working as a professor of sociology when he made his decision to join the revolutionary army. He had studied in Europe and was familiar with the new political theology that was beginning to be written.

There is a directness and honesty about Torres' words:

> It is necessary to take away the power of the privileged minorities in order to give it to the poor majorities. When this is done quickly it creates a revolution. Revolution can be peaceful if the minorities do not resist. Revolution is a way of bringing about a government that feeds the hungry, clothes the naked, instructs the uneducated, carries out works of love for one's neighbour that are not just occasional or transitory and not just for a few but which are for the large majority of our neighbours. That is why the revolution is not only permissible but obligatory for Christians who see in it the only effective way to bring about love for all.[2]

Torres spoke openly about the need for revolution, defining it as a 'fundamental change in economic, social and political structures'. Power had to be taken from the privileged minority and given to the poor majority; that was, according to him, the essence of revolution. His move from word to action anticipated much of what was to become known as liberation theology. He was killed in action within a few weeks of his joining the revolutionary army but he quickly became a symbol for the Latin American Church and an inspiration to many to translate their words into action. In moving from the theory, as a teacher of sociology, to the practice, and in making the supreme sacrifice of his life he 'focused Christianity on effective love for neighbour'. He showed in his life that taking Christ seriously has serious political implications. Few priests followed the same path but his 'willingness to follow his convictions to their ultimate consequences touched the consciences of many Christians'.[3]

Latin American liberation theology has, since then, become a dynamic force within the Catholic Church – causing the Vatican to issue a number of predictable condemnations.

However, the support for liberation theology among some bishops and priests was such that Pope John Paul II felt compelled to write to the Brazilian bishops in 1986:

> The Church does not hesitate to defend fearlessly the just and noble cause of human rights and to support courageous reforms, leading to a better distribution of goods, including earthly goods such as education, health services and so forth ... We are convinced that the theology of liberation is not only timely but useful and necessary. It should constitute a new stage of theological reflection initiated with the apostolic tradition and continued by the great Fathers and Doctors, by the magisterium and by the rich patrimony of the Church's social doctrine.[4]

The Church in Latin America where many – including bishops and priests – have been killed by extreme right wing death squads, trained and financed by the US government, is often called 'the Church of the martyrs'. The growth of liberation theology was perceived as a threat to United States interests in this region. This can be seen in the 1980 Santa Fé Report – a report of a think-tank formulating policy for presidential candidate, Ronald Reagan. The report stated that the United States should work to counter and delegitimise liberation theology as hostile to its own interests: 'US foreign policy must begin to counter liberation theology as it is utilised in Latin America by the "liberation theology" clergy'.

A nominee of President Reagan for Assistant Secretary of State for Human Rights, Ernest Lefever (later rejected by Congress) defined liberation theology 'as a utopian heresy because it sanctified class violence'.[5]

Despite recent changes in eastern Europe, the US Department of State sees itself engaged in a war against communism – 'the third world war', as it is called. It is, in reality, a war against the poor and oppressed and those who work in solidarity with them. This is how one commentator understands it:

> I have come to believe that low-intensity conflict is for the U.S. a global strategy of warfare waged against the poor ... Low-

45

intensity conflict is so broad in scope, so cynical in outlook, so damaging in practice that it presents Christians and Churches ... with a situation similar to that faced by the Confessing Churches in Nazi Germany.[6]

The point about liberation theology is that it demands commitment and participation; it demands action in particular concrete situations of injustice and oppression aimed at overcoming that oppression and restoring power to the poor. Liberation theology does not speak about justice in the abstract. It demands that people be involved in the day to day struggles of the poor. According to liberation theology:

> Christianity places the poor at the centre of human history. And it does so, not only theoretically but practically. Christianity not only interprets history from a point of departure in the liberation of the poor; it sees to it that the poor become actual agents of history ... Christianity is founded on the supposition that no complete, comprehensive science of history can exist. Were such a science to exist Christianity would be superfluous.[7]

Liberation theology insists that the people who are oppressed and downtrodden must be empowered. It is the poor and oppressed themselves who will bring about change and establish justice. Appealing to those in power to grant justice is futile. Education is the key to this empowerment – education as defined by Paulo Freire.[8]

Freire criticises both the traditional form of education and the modernising Church which he says are both aimed at reforming the status quo and making it more acceptable. According to Freire, education is either for conformity or for freedom. Real or authentic education leads to awareness which leads to change. Traditional education based on conformity leads to maintenance of the status quo.

Education is a most important process in any struggle for liberation since in this process people criticise the reality in which they live and discover their power to change it. The education that many have received is the education in seizing and maintaining economic power, in commanding, in using and manipulating other people.

Freire states that the only kind of Church that could be authentic and faithful to the intentions of its founder is a prophetic Church which commits itself to the poor and to radical social change. Freire stresses the importance of leaders who are immersed in the culture and language of the poor and oppressed. He warns against the tendency to treat the oppressed as objects. He points out that many well-intentioned leaders often fall victim to the same methods as used by the oppressor and instead of using the liberation model of dialogue they use the oppressive method of propaganda.

At the Second Vatican Council (1961-65) a highly vocal minority of bishops from the Third World led by Helder Camara lobbied for a 'Church of the poor'. After the Second Vatican Council the official Catholic Church in Latin America made what it called 'a preferential option for the poor'. Base communities – small groups of Christians committed to bringing about social justice – were formed and have grown into a mass movement seeking justice.

At Medellin in 1968 the Latin American bishops denounced 'institutionalised violence' and referred to it as a 'situation of sin'. They called for sweeping changes. They described education as a process that could enable people to become agents of their own advancement. The bishops compared three types of mind-sets: 'Revolutionaries' were described more favourably than 'traditionalists or developmentalists' (who were viewed as technocrats). Revolutionaries were defined as those seeking radical change, those who believed that people should chart their own course.[9]

Pastorally the bishops spelled out a number of commitments, such as defending human rights and carrying out a 'consciousness-raising' mission. They committed the Church to share the condition of the poor out of solidarity. In several places the documents spoke of *communidades de base*, (basic or base communities), a term that had recently been coined to denote small groups of Christians the leader of which was often a layperson. Few such communities existed then but they would soon become widespread.

Priests, religious and lay activists enthusiastically adopted the Medellin documents to justify a completely new pastoral approach. The bishops at Medellin in 1968 saw the base community as the initial cell for building the Church.

The response of the clergy and people to Medellin was affirmed at the Latin American Bishops conference in Puebla in 1972. The Bishops affirmed the preferential option for the poor:

> The love of God ... for us today, must become first and foremost a labour of justice on behalf of the oppressed, an effort of liberation for those who are most in need of it.[10]

The significant point about the growth of this new model of Church is that it had taken place with those who are among the poorest and most marginalised peoples. The very word 'base' is usually understood to mean the 'bottom' of society, that is the poor majority. Such communities have been organised either in rural areas or in the shanty-towns surrounding large cities. It is the poor who feel the need to come together:

> In general base communities have not taken root in middle and upper class Catholicism. These people continue to be served by Catholic schools and parishes not unlike Catholic parishes in Europe and the U.S., as well as by movements (the Cursillo, the Christian Family Movement).[11]

One of the consultants at the Medellin conference was a priest from Peru, Gustavo Gutierrez, who was to become the most influential writer and exponent of the theory behind liberation theology. He stated some years later:

> The concept of the Church of the poor was one of the basic themes Pope John XXIII put forth for the Second Vatican Council ... Giving the poor their decisive place came with the 1968 conference of Latin American bishops at Medellin.[12]

Gutierrez claimed that liberation theology was born just a month before that conference. Referring to his own awakening he stated in another interview:

> I was a Christian, traditionally speaking, from my family and

my school. But to perceive the social side of the Christian message was the beginning of my true Christian commitment.[13]

One of the bishops who attended the Medellin Conference was Helder Camara, who had already become a symbol of the Latin American Church's resistance to injustice and oppression. Both Camara and Gutierrez have shown by their commitment to the poor and their struggle for justice that they believe in the God of the Poor – the God of Life. Their spirituality, based on a firm belief in the work of the Spirit in the struggles of the poor, is not divorced from their everyday lives.

In the context of liberation theology the God of the Poor is very different to the God of the Rich. The God of the Rich is concerned with purely spiritual and legal matters – not with justice and equality. The God of the Rich and powerful calls on the poor to be patient or to accept their lot.

The God of the Poor is different. This God is the God of the Exodus – the God of Life and Hope, often an angry God who led the oppressed people out of slavery in Egypt and conquered their political enemies. The prophets of the Old Testament confronted the political and economic exploitation in a very real way. Like the prophets before him, Jesus of Nazareth challenged the religious and political elites of his day. He too was often angry at the way the poor were treated.

A renewed understanding of the ministry of Jesus has in turn led to a renewed understanding of the mission of the Church, a recovery of the original idea of solidarity with the poor and oppressed. That was lost when the Christian religion became the official religion of the Roman Empire. From then on Church officials were encouraged to become state officials. The Church's interests became identified with those of the state. This brought the Church into disrepute during the Spanish and Portuguese colonisation of Latin America.

Liberation Theology was an attempt to break this alliance of Church and state – an alliance which favoured the rich and powerful to the detriment of the poor. As it has developed over the last 20 years, liberation theology is an attempt to apply the Gospel, understood and interpreted from the situation of the poor, to the situation of inequality and oppression that exists in many countries.

> This means taking sides with labour, women, minority groups, oppressed races, and exploited peoples. It means identifying with the hopes and aspirations of popular culture. Taking sides means confronting the opposing side – the ruling class, dominant culture, landed oligarchy, racist power structures, patriarchal myths and institutions ...[14]

Throughout Latin America there are thousands of small basic Christian communities meeting regularly to reflect, to plan and to celebrate. The basic communities are formed in different ways – with a dialogue course, a Bible circle or through community action and reflection on the Bible. A group may meet to read the Bible, sing, reflect and pray and then go on to discuss the situation of a co-operative, or go out to fix a road so that buses and lorries can get to the village.

The members of the basic communities, mostly poor people, are once again putting the Bible in its proper place, the place where God intended it to be – in second place. Life and the situation of the poor takes first place. In so doing the people are showing us the enormous importance of the Bible and at the same time its relative value – in relation to life. So 'when they read the Bible they are not trying to interpret the Bible; they are trying to interpret life with the help of the Bible. The people are taking back their book from the clergy.'[15]

The Church in the Philippines has experienced a similar growth of basic Christian communities. One activist describes the process:

> Casting one's lot with the poor is the most basic element of the entire process of Christian community building ... But what do we mean by casting ones lot with the poor? ... It is fundamentally a matter of standpoint ... whom do we serve ... the poor or big businessmen? ... And since it is in the highest interests of the poor to struggle for sovereignty, democracy, social progress, and full humanity, to serve them is to serve their just

and legitimate struggle ... by the poor we do not simply mean the poor in the abstract or the poor in sociology books, or the poor as objects of welfare assistance, but the great majority of the Filipino people, who suffer because they are poor and suffer because they struggle.[16]

For all those engaged in pastoral work, it is faith in the God of the Poor that is the important reality. Gustavo Gutierrez, speaking in 1984, stated that although he considers his theological perspective important, it is secondary to 'prayer, worship, contemplation and commitment'. The truly important thing is the concrete commitment to the poor as set out in the Gospels. For him the root of his life is his faith in Jesus Christ, not liberation theology.[17]

As a result of this commitment to the poor, in some countries, a greater appreciation of popular religion – the faith and practices of the people – has developed within the basic communities.

If, for example people are systematically prevented from having any real power, it is not surprising that they seek powerful advocates in heaven. If many people without access to modern medicine see their children die, it is not surprising that they should see infant baptism as a possible remedy for illness. In fact, since colonial times religion has enabled people to hold up and resist under very difficult conditions and to make sense out of life.[18]

In practice, according to one observer, John Berryman, respect for the people's religious faith came to mean listening before teaching, seeking to understand and then helping people themselves come to a critical awareness of their own religious traditions and practices. He gives examples of how a community might decide to change its traditional practices. For example, a community might make a conscious collective decision to control or eliminate alcohol on a patron saint's feast, not out of narrowly moralistic reasons but because they were being exploited by the liquor manufacturers and because when they got drunk they were disfiguring the image of God within them. In other cases they might put a new, more biblical interpretation on an existing practice. Thus, a procession might be seen as a symbol of the ancient Exodus from Egypt and the march towards liberation today.[19]

The development of liberation theology with the growth of basic Christian communities has created tension within the Catholic Church. There are the two tendencies – one supported by the Vatican and its political allies, which seeks to maintain the status the Church has held traditionally in society, and the other which opts for social change by supporting grassroots organisations. This conflict has spilled over into the public arena.

In Nicaragua after the 1979 revolution the bishops did not accept a new role for the Church. They adhered to the old paternalistic Church because of their unwillingness to accept that the Sandinista government had been recognised by the people as an alternative source of moral authority.[20]

The bishops feared a split in the Church in Nicaragua. Their fears were not without foundation, though the base communities had affirmed their commitment to work for unity in the Church and denied that there is such a thing as a 'popular Church' outside the mainstream Church. In 1984 the Nicaraguan bishops stated that a small part of the Church had abandoned ecclesiastical unity and was sowing confusion by extolling its own ideas and slandering the legitimate pastors. In their Easter 1986 pastoral letter, they sharply attacked what they called the 'popular Church' for actively undermining the foundations upon which the unity of the Catholic Church is built.

Pope John Paul II also shared their concern about disunity. He wrote in 1982: 'The unity of the faithful must be concretely woven around the bishop. Without him this unity does not exist or is falsified.' The Pope took a dim view of the fact that four priests were serving in the Sandinista government and ordered them to choose either their posts or their active ministry. One of them, Ferdinando Cardenal wrote:

Our service to God in the priesthood has led us to the ministry of charity and love, which in Nicaragua has been translated into a ministry in support of the forward march of the people, the ministry of accompanying our people from within, by participating in a transformation of structures, so that the poor may have justice.[21]

It was clear that the priests in government and the Pope and bishops had radically different models of Church. For Pope John Paul II the most appropriate role for the Church to play in society appears to be one based on a version of the old Christendom model where the Church and state, though independent of each other, collaborate and legitimate one another.[22]

The priests in the Nicaraguan government did not see their relationship with the civil authorities in the same way as the Pope. They described their involvement in a revolutionary government as 'serving the people' and, as such, symbolic of the Church's renunciation of its past alliances with ruling elites. As far as the Pope was concerned their complete identification with a civil government compromised the Church and sacrificed its independent authority.[23]

In fact the Pope was not taking the position of opposing political liberation or the preferential option for the poor as such and on his visits to Latin America he has repeatedly affirmed the Church's commitment to the cause of justice and its solidarity with the needy and the suffering: 'You rightly feel – and should always feel – the longing for a more just society,' he told a gathering of Peruvian Christians during a visit there in February 1985, 'but do not follow those who say that social injustice can only disappear through hatred between the classes or the resort to violence or other anti-Christian methods.'

Those who identify with the poor or who make a 'preferential option for the poor' know the risks they are taking – both from the extreme right-wing in politics and and the reactionary elements within the Church. They are once again taking the same risks that the early Christians took. The recovery of the Gospel of freedom has given many the inspiration to take up the cause of the poor and oppressed irrespective of the consequences to themselves.

The priests in the government of Nicaragua, which has since gone out of office after losing the 1989 election, issued the following response in 1981 to an ultimatum from the bishops insisting that they resign from political office or face ecclesiastical sanctions:

> We believe in God the father, Creator of the world and human beings. We believe in Jesus Christ, the son of God, our brother and our Saviour. We believe in the Church, the visible body of Christ to which we belong. We believe in justice, the basis of human community and communion. We believe in love, the first and principal commandment of Jesus. We believe in our priesthood which is our vocation to serve our brothers and sisters. We believe in our country, that great family to which we belong and to which we owe our being. We believe in the Nicaraguan people's revolution, fashioned by the people in order to overthrow tyranny and sow justice and love. We believe in the poor, who will be the ones to build a more just homeland, and who will help us to be saved ourselves. This is our faith and our hope.[24]

The priests were declaring that building the reign of God is not done simply by liturgical celebrations or by talking about it. The real work must be done in the political and in the social sphere. Those who say it is better to stay out of politics are, in fact, by their silence supporting, condoning and legitimising the unjust system. Those who say the Church should be neutral have already taken sides.

In a real sense, then, a new Church is being born in some countries, a Church which is not authoritarian and distant, a Church which is not aligned with the rich and powerful – but a Church of the poor where the concerns and problems of the poor – especially of women and children – are of the first importance to all the members and officials in the Church. This birth has not been easy. There has been strong resistance from within the Church as well as from military and political elites. We have seen in Haiti the extent to which these will go, when a duly elected President who was also a priest working with the poor, had to flee the country. Since then the Vatican has recognised the new military dictatorship.

Each time the Gospel is preached in an authentic manner, it encounters fanatical resistance, not least in the interior of the Churches. The Church is holy, but within it there implant themselves cabals, interest groups, synagogues of Satan. But in the end the Christian conscience will always remember that the human beings of the whole world, whatever their race or colour of their skin, are immortal beings created in the image of God, children of one God and brothers and sisters of each other, including their torturers. We stand in a Biblical pattern – that of Cain and Abel. Fratricidal wars do exist; and they are abominable to the degree that they are fratricidal. Thanks to the theology of Las Casas, in the place of justice at least there remained remorse in the Christian conscience, and consequently repentance was possible. The results have not been as meagre as they might seem.[25]

With the collapse of authoritarian structures in many places in recent years some believe that the days of the authoritarian Church are numbered. The old autocratic Church is being challenged to become a new democratic, people-centred Church. This internal struggle to create a new Church will continue to gain momentum in the years to come. But there are still many in positions of power determined to resist change.

The struggle for democracy within the Catholic Church has immense implications for the clergy – the bishops and priests. Not many will take the decision to follow the way of Camillo Torres. But all are called to be authentic preachers and witnesses to the Gospel in the midst of injustice and oppression. Church leaders have a special responsibility not to say or do anything which would undermine the struggles of the poor and oppressed or lead to further repression.

Liberation theology offers the Church a positive way forward so that it can be immediately identified with the struggles of the poor:

The uniqueness to which liberation theology lays claim is that of being a faith reflection originating and developing within the actual practice of liberation. Let me be very clear; liberation theology is not a reflection on the theoretical subject of liberation. It is a reflection on the concrete practice of liberation engaged in by the poor and by their allies in struggle.[26]

55

There are a number of different theologies within the Church – traditional/conservative; liberal theology which is in favour of reforming the political and economic status quo; and liberation theology which originates with the poor and oppressed in their struggle for justice and freedom. Is it any wonder then that liberation theology has met with such hostility and criticism from those in positions of power both in Church and State as well as those with a vested interest in maintaining the status quo? Liberation theology is first of all committed to action. For that reason those in power and in control perceive it as a threat to their interests and their control. There are those in the Church who are afraid of liberation theology because they are afraid of equality. However, the liberation theology movement has become so strong and so deeply rooted that it cannot now be stopped or undermined.

4

From Celtic to Roman: A Brief History of the Irish Church

Irish Celtic Christianity had a tendency towards monasticism from the beginning ... Ireland became unique in western Christendom in having its most important Churches ruled by a monastic hierarchy many of whom were not bishops. In fact a monastic system replaced dioceses altogether (Tomás Ó Fiaich, *Course of Irish History*).

The first Christian missionaries to Ireland did not attempt a root and branch eradication of the Celtic druidic tradition and beliefs. Instead, the new religion absorbed the holy mountains and the innumerable holy wells and gave them a Christian name. (It has been estimated that there were approximately 3,000 holy wells some of which, like Doon well in Donegal, remain in use). This popular or vernacular religion separate and distinct from the institutional hierarchical Church has, from the outset, been a vibrant characteristic of Irish Christianity.

There is evidence that the native Celts worshipped nature gods – one of whom was Manaman Mac Lir, god of the sea. They worshipped in rituals prescribed by the Druids – the religious teachers. The Druids believed very firmly in the after-life:

> Death is only a changing of place and life goes on with its forms and goods in another world, a world of the dead which gives up the living. Therefore, a constant exchange of souls takes place between the two worlds: death in this world brings a soul to the other and death in the other brings a soul to this one. Julius Caesar observed that this religious outlook account-

57

ed for the reckless bravery of the Celts in battle, with their apparent complete lack of fear of death.[1]

It is easy to see how the Resurrection story would have appealed to them. The Druids were the philosophers of society. Aristotle stated that much early Greek philosophy was borrowed from them. The Druids were also historians and educators, organising schools and higher education. They were political advisers, exempt from military service and allowed to travel the country freely.

The soul-friend (*anam chara*) who acted as a spiritual guide and counsellor – not confessor – to young monks and converts was part of Druidic practice. The Christian abbots of the Celtic settlements were later to adopt the same practice of soul-friend or *anam chara*. The first Christian priests also adopted the druidic tonsure which shaved the front of the head from ear to ear; they wore similar white robes and carried an identical staff or crook. Columba could refer to Christ as 'his Druid'. The Druids retained their status as wise men and counsellors well into the Christian era.

The early Christian Church also absorbed reverence for the natural environment from the prior Druidic veneration of the earth seen especially in their ritual gatherings in oak groves. The modern city of Derry (Doire) derives from an early Christian monastery located in an earlier druidic site.

Christianity was established in Ireland in the early fifth century, even before St Patrick came in 432 AD. It may have first come to Ireland through Egyptian, Jewish or Coptic sources. It was established according to the monastic tradition which, it is said, originated in Egypt and had been adopted by Christianity and developed alongside the episcopal Church. This monastic way of life was based on seclusion. The monks dedicated themselves to prayer and penance and took vows of poverty, chastity and obedience. The native Irish were attracted to this ascetic way of life, perhaps because the organisation was similar to that in the *tuatha*.

A large number of monasteries were established throughout Ireland – some in very remote places, where the monks took seriously the Gospel instruction of Jesus; 'any of you who does not give up everything cannot be my disciple' (Lk. 14:33). They hoped to escape the influences of material life. Sceilig Mhichil, off the Kerry coast, is a well known example. These monasteries became like estates, directed to a religious purpose but with only a small number actually leading the lifestyle of the hermit. The abbot was often married and was succeeded by his offspring.

It was this Celtic form of Christianity that the Irish monks in turn brought with them throughout Europe when in the sixth century Columbanus led the way to those who left their homes for purely ascetic reasons. These were the 'peregrini' – pilgrims undertaking the *perigrinatio pro Christi*. It was a voluntary exile undertaken in order to become close to Christ. Wherever they went they were to influence those with whom they lived, caring for the needs of the poor and the sick.

The early Irish Church reflected the society in which it developed. Irish society in the fifth and sixth centuries was decentralised. It was a loose federation of about 150 small independent states (*tuatha*) with a population of about half a million people. Ireland had not been colonised by Rome – one of the few European countries to escape – and so retained its own native decentralised form of self-government.

The early monasteries adapted to this social system. The Christian Church in Ireland almost from its inception was different from the Roman hierarchical and centralised Church which developed throughout Europe with the expansion of the Roman empire. The Roman Church was closely linked to cities and urbanism, whereas the Celtic Church remained rural in focus and organisation.

Early Celtic Christianity, therefore, may have had more in common with Eastern philosophy than with the institutional Christianity of the West. The Christian religion blended well with Irish religious faith and with the Celtic social system. The land was owned in common by kin or extended families as is seen in the Brehon laws. These families adopted the Christian faith and set up small monastic centres based on Christian principles. 'Monasteries were not made up only of scholars and ascetics. They were part of society, close to their own kin.'[2]

The monastic schools of the Celtic Church developed from the druidical colleges and the influence of the Egyptian movement of Christian hermits who sought quiet places for their cells. The lives of the saints give many accounts of men who went into the monastic schools in Ireland for a period of twenty years, the length of time taken to train a druid. The training which involved the commitment of long passages to memory was similar to druidic training.[3] It is probable that (as in Britain) many monasteries were actually founded on sites of druid colleges.

The early Celtic Church of the fifth and sixth centuries was organised around monasteries and abbeys controlled not by bishops but by abbots or abbesses. St Patrick had introduced the episcopal Church. Bishops had simply a liturgical function – preaching, ordaining priests and celebrating the sacraments.

As well as the organisational difference between the Irish Church and the Roman Church there was a radically different Celtic theology. There was a greater emphasis on social equality and on respect for the earth and the environment – in modern parlance, a greater ecological awareness. The sense of God's presence in nature is evident in early Gaelic poetry:

> There sings to me a cuckoo
> from bush-citadels in grey hood.
> God's doom! May the Lord protect me
> writing well under the great wood.[4]

In the Celtic monastic Church the persons of Jesus and Mary were highly respected. The main events in their lives were celebrated throughout the year. It was in the person of Jesus of Nazareth that the true God, as the God of the poor and oppressed, is revealed. The honour for his mother reflected the early Celtic Christians' belief that Jesus learned this sensitivity and compassion for the poor and marginalised from his mother, herself a marginalised person. It was Jesus who revealed the true God as the God of the Poor and the kind of society that this God wants – a society where all God's family are equal, where none are marginalised or treated as second class citizens.

Within the early Celtic Church there is evidence that women were accorded equal terms with men. Women's rights were already protected in the Brehon laws established by the early Celtic inhabitants of Ireland. It is suggested by some historians that women participated in the celebration of Mass – much to the displeasure of the Roman authorities.

The independence expressed by the early Christian Church in Ireland and its absorption of elements of the older Celtic religion and customs were frowned upon by the authorities in Rome. Pope John in 634 AD wrote to the Irish denouncing their independence from Rome. Patrick had attempted to establish an episcopal Church but this soon yielded to a monastic Church which seemed to suit the localised Irish Celtic social system based on the clan or extended family.

The new Church was tied into the existing social structures which were built around the local ruler and his 'erenach' – the hereditary custodian of Church lands. The Church's land was called the termon. Thus we have the origins of some of the present parishes – Termonmagrath, Termonmagurk etc. There are many references in the *Annals* to the close relationship between the Church and the clan. In Fermanagh, for example, local families like Muldoon, McManus and Cassidy became protectors of local Churches and parish clergy. This close relationship survived intact until English colonial conquest destroyed this social system of local control during the last years of the sixteenth and early seventeenth centuries.

Various reasons have been offered for the strong preference among the Irish for a monastic-type Church which submerged the diocesan system. The diocesan system was imported from Rome and was largely dependent on an urban system to work effectively. Celtic custom with regard to inheritance and kinship could survive much better having much more local support. The significance of the close relations between the rural-based laity and the monastery is seen in the common Celtic word for a people or a community, *muintir*, which derives from the Latin *monasterium*.[5]

Tension continued between the Pope and the Irish Celtic Church (and its sister Celtic Church in Britain) throughout the sixth and seventh centuries. There was a long-running dispute about the date of Easter. However the main point at issue between the Celtic Church and the Church in Rome was power and the administration of power:

> For the Celts, bishops (including the bishop of Rome) were valuable executive officials but as such they did not have the spiritual authority invested in the abbots, many of whom presided over institutions founded by themselves and who gathered disciples and converts around them. It was a dispensation fitting to rural communities, who expected to conduct their affairs in small groups and in comparative isolation. But it was intolerable to a quasi-military power which needed to control its institutions through an inflexible network of communications.[6]

The Celtic Church which developed throughout Ireland between 400-1100 served the people well. To judge by surviving monuments in stone and bronze as well as in the literature this was a vibrant, open and creative Church. The Round Towers and High Crosses showed exquisite workmanship and devotion. The illuminated manuscripts like the *Book of Kells* (eighth century) demonstrate a remarkable skill in artistic design and calligraphy and reflected the high esteem in which the Scriptures were held at the time.

The monasteries attracted students from all over Europe to study religion and medicine. Anglo-Saxons came to Ireland to study the religious life and, according to Venerable Bede, the Irish 'welcomed them all gladly'. Aldfrith who became King of Northumbria in 685 AD was educated in County Fermanagh at Lisgoole on the shores of the Erne. The better known monastic foundations were Monasterboice, founded about 500 AD, Clonard also founded about the year 500 AD by Finian, and Aran, founded by Enda. Finian is credited with preparing many other monks to found monasteries – including Colmcille of Derry, Molaisse of Devenish, Ninidh of Inismacsaint, and Ciaran of Clonmacnoise.

> The monasteries, in addition to their primary religious purpose, were places for fosterage and centres of education and learning. They also fulfilled another important social function since they provided patronage for the arts.[7]

Irish monks spread Christianity and learning through the Anglo-Saxon kingdoms. Iona and Lindisfarne became known as the 'Athens of the North'. Irish monks travelled as far as Iceland, Italy and the Ukraine. This period, it must be remembered, was known in Europe as 'the Dark Ages' because of the wars and desolation wrought by the barbarian invasions of Western Europe. Ireland alone kept intact the tradition of European learning in the monastic schools and then re-exported it back to Europe through its missionaries.

The Irish monasteries provided a full religious and educational service to the people who lived in small rural communities – often moving from place to place. The liturgy and the sacraments were available. The monastery was open to the people to visit and to pray at all times. Those who needed shelter for the night found lodgings there. The monks practised hospitality as an essential virtue for all who would be disciples – in fact St Molaisse's monastery at Devenish in Fermanagh was known as 'the House of Hospitality'. The Round Towers or belfries summoned the people to the Church services. The monasteries became centres of commerce and functioned as craft centres. They also served as open prisons for persistent offenders against society.

The Church in mainland Europe took a different course. As the feudal system of ownership gained ground, the Church based in Rome followed suit. It became increasingly worldly and concerned with acquiring land, wealth and power. In England the Roman system gained the ascendancy after 664 AD. At the Synod of Whitby, Roman and Celtic Christians met to discuss their differences; the Romans won the day. Britain was soon to be conquered by the Normans. The Celtic Church in Ireland was now in grave danger of becoming Romanised as well.

Even before the Anglo-Normans invaded Ireland in 1169 a movement had begun within the Irish Church arguing for the adoption of the Roman feudal system which involved a more centralised and hierarchical form of government. In support of this the pro-Roman Churchmen cited certain Celtic customs relating to marriage and cohabitation and laws permitting divorce, as evidence that the Irish were not true Christians and needed to be brought into line. Malachy, the newly appointed archbishop of Armagh, stated after his appointment that:

> It was not to men but to beasts he had been sent; in all the barbarism which he had yet encountered, he never met such a people so profligate in their morals, so uncouth in their ceremonies, so impious in faith, so barbarous in laws, so rebellious to discipline, so filthy in life, Christian in name but Pagan in reality.

Malachy's view of the situation did not go unquestioned. When he started to build an elaborate Church in Bangor, one inhabitant protested that it was a needless frivolity for 'we are Irish not Gauls'.

The Anglo-Normans, led by Henry II, who invaded Ireland in 1169 shared Malachy's sentiments and presented their invasion as a religious mission when in fact it was a political one taking advantage of a local dispute. King Henry received the blessing of the Pope Alexander II for the conquest. The Bull *Laudabiliter* given to Henry by the English-born Pope Adrian IV (Nicholas Breakspeare) in 1155 stated that the Normans were coming to conquer Ireland so as to 'enlarge the boundaries of the Church, to proclaim the truths of the Christian religion to a rude and ignorant people and to root out the growths of vice from the field of the Lord'.

Such justification for conquest and persecution on religious grounds was common in Europe at the time. The Christian Crusades used the same pretext for their attacks on Palestine in the eleventh and twelfth centuries.[8]

Henry II, who had just taken part in the killing of Archbishop Thomas a Beckett, received the approval of two

Popes for his act of aggression in Ireland. Thus began the first systematic colonial conquest of Ireland by the neighbouring power in England. By 1172 the English had secured most of the high Church offices in Ireland and considered the first stage of conquest a success.

However, the Norman invasion did not have the same lasting consequences for Ireland as the second colonial conquest in the sixteenth and seventeenth centuries when the English Reformation introduced the factor of religious persecution. The Normans brought to Ireland their well-known skills for organisation – which was what the Vatican wanted in order that the Church would be centralised and under the direct control of a hierarchy, as in Italy and throughout the rest of Europe. The Vatican authorities believed that certain abuses in the Church with regard to marriage, patronage, etc were the result of the absence of a highly centralised authority structure.

> The biggest and most active agency in preparing the way for the feudalisation of Ireland and the invasion of the Anglo-Normans was the Roman Church.[9]

The Normans brought to Ireland the feudal system of local ownership and political control. Under feudalism the Church became part of the state apparatus at the local as well as the national level. The urban took precedence over the rural and centralised government was intended to replace decentralised local government – which had been the practice in Ireland.

This process took many decades and really only took deep root in the Pale – the area of the country under Norman control. Large areas of Munster, Ulster and Connacht still retained the Gaelic way of life. It was mainly in the Norman-ruled part of Ireland that the continental religious orders – Cistercians, Augustinians, etc – organised. The Franciscans, however, organised mainly throughout Gaelic Ireland.

***

The Pope who issued Henry II with the *Laudabiliter* in 1155 seems to have ignored the efforts of the Irish clergy to bring about internal reform in the Irish Church. They had held a series of synods culminating in the Synod of Kells in 1152. The impetus for this reform movement had, indeed, come from Rome, which had received reports of a disorganised Church. With this reorganisation the Church was brought more into line with the Church in the rest of Europe.

These reforms were carried out under two local archbishops of Armagh – Cellach and Malachy. In 1111 a national synod held at Rath Breasail near Cashel, County Tipperary presided over by the primate and the high king, divided Ireland into episcopal sees intended to replace the monastic organisation. The monasteries were gradually brought under diocesan control. The reforms meant the end of the decentralised and democratic-type Church that had been established in Ireland in the fifth and sixth centuries.

From then on the Roman authorities were to keep a much tighter rein on the Irish Church:

> At repeated intervals Alexander III, Innocent III, Honorius III and John XXII issued warnings to the clergy and people of Ireland about their duty of obedience to the king of England.[10]

The reform movement which began at Rath Breasail in 1111 concluded with the Synod of Kells in 1152. Most of the newly appointed bishops were members of Anglo-Norman families attached to Canterbury and they, rather than the local abbot, became the most important Churchmen in the local area. Nevertheless, outside of the Pale (Counties Dublin, Meath, Kildare and Louth) which was now controlled by the Normans, the new religious orders from Europe, especially the Franciscans, began to play an important role in the social and religious life of the Irish people. This role lasted until most of them were suppressed by Henry VIII in the early sixteenth century.

From the twelfth century onwards English perceptions of the native Irish were influenced by travellers who came over from Britain with the Normans and who wrote about the country. One of these was an influential Churchman from Wales, Giraldus Cambrensis who first travelled to Ireland in 1183 to report on the condition of the Irish Church. His book, *History and Topography of Ireland* (dedicated to Henry II) written in 1185, was to become the main source book for English 'historians' for centuries afterwards. The following extracts give a flavour of his writing and thinking:

> This is a filthy people wallowing in vice. Of all people it is the least instructed in the rudiments of the faith ... they are a wild and inhospitable people. They live on beasts only and they live like beasts. They have not progressed at all from the primitive habits of pastoral living.[11]

These writings were enough to justify for the colonists the righteousness of their mission to Ireland. The racist diatribe of Giraldus of Wales was quoted for centuries afterwards by historians as fact.[12]

While the Normans superficially succeeded in conquering three-quarters of the country the native Irish population resisted their foreign ways and customs. The Anglo-Normans gradually adapted to the Irish ways and became 'more Irish than the Irish themselves'. The English crown continued its efforts to conquer and control the whole country – mainly for strategic reasons – but without lasting success. The resisitance movement was too strong and involved all sections of Irish society. A joint force of Scots and Irish under Edward Bruce reversed the Ulster plantations in 1314.

The Church in most of the country continued to organise around monasteries and remained an independent institution closely involved in the lives of the people not as a controlling agent – but as a social institution of support and a promoter of learning. There were abuses within the Church in Ireland as elsewhere particularly in regard to patronage. It was the abuses with regard to money, indulgences and patronage which precipitated the Protestant Reformation in northern Europe led by an Augustinian monk Martin Luther (1483-1546) and the Swiss writer Calvin (1509-1564). The Protestant Reformation was adopted in England by Henry VIII (1509-1547) who was also in dispute with the Pope because of the Vatican's refusal to allow him to remarry. Henry determined that he and not the Pope should henceforth be the head of the Church.

Up until the reign of Henry VIII (1509-1547) there were two political systems in Ireland: one Norman and the other Gaelic. The parliament in Dublin controlled by the Anglo-Irish and the Old English had no control over Gaelic Ireland. Those parts of Ulster ruled by the O'Neills, the Maguires and the O'Donnells were 'no go areas' for the English. The Tudors set out to change that and to create a centralised government whose writ would run over the whole country. They had tried to do the same within Britain itself attempting to take complete control of Scotland. This was the era of expansion with the discovery of the Americas and the vast resources of wealth to be had from the taking over of these countries. England was now competing with Spain for a share in these spoils.

This period – the sixteenth century – marked the transition from feudalism to capitalism. If there was to be a strong capitalist state there was need for strong centralised government. Capitalists need bigger areas to control and more centralisation of the economy. They need military control as well as administrative and economic control. The Tudor and Elizabethan rulers saw the need to bring the whole island of Ireland – especially Ulster where there was the strongest Gaelic resistance – under their control. In order to achieve this they sent over a strong army and reorganised these territories into counties with their own justices and jails.

The second colonisation of Ireland began in 1541 when the Dublin Parliament changed Henry VIII's title from 'Lord of Ireland' to 'King of Ireland'. This colonial conquest continued until 1650 when Oliver Cromwell, the leader of the Puritan party in England which had routed King Charles, brought the whole country under English domination. The Cromwellians confiscated most of the land and handed it over to those who backed the war financially and who subscribed to the Protestant Reformation. Cromwell declared his purpose to be a 'great work against the barbarous and blood-thirsty Irish and the rest of their adherents and confederates, for the propagation of the Gospel of Christ, the establishing of truth and peace, and restoring that bleeding nation to its former happiness and tranquillity.'[13]

It was in the context of the growth of Catholic Spain as an imperial power that English monarchs and parliamentarians saw the need to gain control of all of Catholic Ireland. A Protestant government of a Protestant country could not accept the potential threat posed by a Catholic, and therefore, subversive people in neighbouring Ireland. The religion of the people, it was decreed, had to be the religion of the monarch. That was the practice throughout Europe after the Reformation. The declared intentions of the English rulers, were to civilise the Irish and convert them to become civilised English-speaking Protestants, and thereby remove the strategic threat of an alliance between Catholic Spain and Catholic Ireland.

However, the close ties that had been built between the Church and the Irish people – all sections of Irish society – throughout the fourteenth and fifteenth centuries meant that when the Reformation came to Ireland with Henry VIII in 1530 its attempts to pervert the Gaelic Irish or the Old English to Protestantism met strong resistance. This new form of Christianity involved recognition of the King/Queen of England – not the Pope – as head of the Church. The Roman Catholic religion practised by 80% of the Irish people now became (or was perceived as) another element of resistance to the English conquest.

The English colonists in the 1500s and 1600s justified their colonial conquest using standard colonial pretexts; they argued that the Irish were culturally inferior and superstitious and that the English would civilise them. They condemned Irish religious practices, criticising them for failing even to practise Catholicism properly! Spenser had written that the native Irish 'all be papists by their profession, but in the same so blindly and brutishly uninformed (for the most part) that not one amongst a hundred knoweth any ground of Religion or any article of his faith.'[14] Another writer remarked about the Irish: 'They are more foolish, super-

69

stitious in Ireland than they can be in Rome itself.' The English classed the Irish as 'barbarians' who had missed out on the supposed benefits of Roman colonisation.

In promoting ideas about the cultural inferiority of the Irish the colonisers after 1560 were following similar logic to that of their Spanish counterparts in South America. By treating the native peoples as inferior, barbaric and inhuman, the colonists legitimised murder, theft and in the case of the Amerindians mass extermination.

In the reign of Henry VIII (1509-1547) an onslaught was made on the monasteries. Church lands were confiscated and given to those landlords who swore their allegiance to the crown. There was some respite during the reigns of Edward VI (1547-1553) and Mary (1553-58) but when Elizabeth I (1558-1603) came to the throne there began another period of severe persecution of those who did not subscribe to the Protestant faith and the English crown. It was during the reign of Elizabeth I (1558-1603) that many clergy, including some bishops, were killed by the English forces.

It was in this period that the Irish bard MacCoistealbha wrote 'Mo Roisín Dubh' (My Dark Rosaleen):

O my dark Rosaleen
Do not sigh do not weep!
The priests are on the ocean green,
They march along the deep.
There's wine from the royal Pope,
Upon the ocean green;
And Spanish ale shall give you hope,
My Dark Rosaleen!
My Dark Rosaleen!

With the counter-Reformation in the early years of the seventeenth century the Catholic Church in Ireland began to be re-organised. Dioceses without bishops were filled and twenty colleges, for the education of priests, were opened on the Continent.

In 1642 Catholic Churchmen, including an Italian, Rinuccini sent over by the Vatican, joined forces with the Irish chiefs in the Confederation of Kilkenny to attempt to recover their lands and re-establish the supremacy of the Catholic faith. They professed their allegiance to the English King, Charles II, then under threat from the parliament. Their motto was 'Ireland united for God, king and country'. But they were not united and so they were easily defeated when the parliamentary forces that had defeated Charles II were able to concentrate on dealing with the Irish rebel armies.

By 1650 the English army under Cromwell had succeeded in suppressing almost the entire native Irish resistance – at a tremendous cost in terms of human life. The atrocities committed by Cromwell helped forge close links between the native Irish people and the Old English – the name given to those descendants of the first Norman-English settlers, Fitzgeralds, Butlers, Burkes, etc, who had become 'more Irish than the Irish'.

Cromwell's campaign was regarded as an attempt not only to take over the land but to suppress forever the Catholic religion in Ireland – so that there would no longer be any threat on that front. The Cromwellian war of conquest is remembered for the ruthless sectarian attacks on the Catholic people, their Churches and their monasteries and for the massacres at Drogheda and Wexford.

Throughout the sixteenth and seventeenth centuries, Ireland was a theatre for the wider European conflict sparked by the Reformation and counter-Reformation. Protestant England vied with Catholic Spain for superiority in the world – especially in the new world of the Americas. So long as the English failed to subjugate the Catholic Irish so long England would regard the Irish nation as a strategic threat: Ireland could be used as a back-door by the Spanish to launch an invasion.

English policy with regard to Ireland from the Tudor period (1509 onwards) was aimed at conquest. This meant the dispossession of those who refused to conform to the English/Protestant establishment and the suppression of the Catholic faith. 'Popery' was politically suspect; the new aristocracy in Ireland established an exclusively Protestant parliament in Dublin. The Protestant Church became the established Church – even though it represented only 10 per cent of the people. As far as the Protestant aristocracy was concerned the single greatest threat to their power and the English connection was still the strength of the Catholic Church in Ireland. Even after 1690-91 when James II and his forces were routed at the Boyne and sent into exile in France, they feared the continuing allegiance of the Irish people to Jacobitism – the movement to return the Catholic family of James to the English throne.

Penal Laws[15] were passed by the exclusively Protestant Dublin parliament from 1691 onwards in an attempt to reduce the power and influence of Catholics and the Catholic Church. Their aims were fourfold: i) to break up the estates still in the hands of Catholic landlords and simultaneously prevent them from acquiring any additional real property; ii) to exclude Catholics from any role in government, either national or local; iii) to bar them from the professions, civil or military; iv) to raise serious impediments to Catholic worship so that eventually Catholicism in Ireland would wither away.

The impact of this attack on the Catholic Church in Ireland was to fuse the varying strands within Ireland into a community of the dispossessed. It fostered a strong sense of shared suffering – especially after Cromwell, when Catholicism became in effect a vast 'trade union of the dispossessed'.

By the late 1600s the Irish – both Gaelic and Norman – were almost completely dispossessed of their land and homes. Even after the deliberate policy of plantation had ended, the influx of settlers, from Scotland in particular, continued into the early years of the eighteenth century. The vast majority of the Irish – many living in poverty – remained loyal to the Catholic Church with the support of the clergy. Throughout this period of oppression and persecution one religious order of clergy, the Franciscans, remained particularly close to the people. They had come to Ireland as early as 1226. They had established their monasteries in the Gaelic areas and brought with them the basic spirituality of Saint Francis of Assisi with its strong emphasis on simplicity of lifestyle. This was welcomed by the native Irish who had a long tradition of similar spirituality. Many Franciscans were to be killed by the English authorities.

There were some within the Protestant tradition – like Jonathon Swift, Dean of St Patrick's Cathedral, and Bishop George Berkeley of Cloyne – who objected to the treatment of the Catholic population and the social and economic conditions. Swift advocated Irish independence from England as the best solution.

However, as the policies of the English government failed to have the desired effect of turning the people away from the Catholic faith and as the Jacobite threat disappeared, the English government increasingly saw the Irish Catholic hierarchy as its most effective means of controlling the Irish people. It was encouraged in this belief by the rapidly-changing political situation in Europe – especially in France – which brought about a closer relationship between the Court of St James in London and the Vatican.

Statements made by Irish bishops reflected the change of policy by the English authorities towards the official Catholic Church – a policy which did not extend to the bulk of the members. The bishops believed that by adopting a more servile, fawning approach they would reassure the English authorities of their loyalty (and the loyalty of their obedient flocks) and help bring about a change from a persecuted Church to a Church which was acceptable to, and tolerated by, the State. By 1762, even though the Penal Laws were still on the statute books, we find in a pastoral letter issued by Bishop O'Brien of Cloyne to the clergy of the diocese the first sign of a shift in policy by a loyal Church hierarchy:

Reverend Sirs,
I have lately sent directions to all those amongst you who are situated on the frontiers of the neighbouring counties, that have been infested with those profligate disturbers of the public peace and tranquillity, who are called 'white boys' or 'levellers', to exhort and admonish the good people of their respective congregations, against having any hand, or taking the least part, directly or indirectly, in any illegal practices, or

holding any sort of conduct, that might give offence to the government, especially in the recent general conjecture of troublesome times, when all the Roman Catholics of this kingdom should rather be more attentive than ever, to manifest their unfeigned dispositions of giving our most excellent and noble-minded lieutenant, and all our other great and good governors, the best and most solid proofs in our power, of the just and grateful feeling we have, and always should have of their lenity and indulgence towards us in our unhappy circumstances, subjected as we are, according to the disposition of providence, not only to legal restraints and incapacities, but also to penal laws, whose weight and severity,we already find to be alleviated in great measure, through the goodness and clemency of our most gracious rulers ... After these charitable admonishments to your respective flocks on this occasion, I hereby desire and order that you will publish and issue out in all forms, an excommunication, to be incurred de facto by all those of your communion, who should happen to have engaged or acted in those parties of iniquity and works of darkness.[16]

This pastoral set the tone for other pastorals from Irish bishops up until and after the 1798 Rising.

***

Until the French Revolution in 1789, leaders of the Protestant Ascendancy in Ireland believed that Catholics could never make decisions independently of their clergy and hierarchy – and thus could not be trusted in government. They suspected the power of Rome and feared persecution at the hands of Catholics. These fears lay behind the introduction of the Penal laws. Catholics could not be allowed to have a say in government because, it was feared, they would act only on instructions from Rome.

But the French Revolution showed that Catholics were no longer subject to the Church's control or afraid of the Church's power. Catholics in France led the attack on the clergy as well as the monarchy. The French Revolution showed Protestants that Catholics were capable of acting independently of their clergy and hierarchy. This had obvious implications for Ireland. If French Catholics were showing political maturity, then perhaps, so too could Irish Catholics.

The French Revolution led to the spread of radical ideas among sections of the Presbyterian and Anglican community in Ireland during the 1790s – ideas about political and economic organisation and the redistribution of wealth. Through the United Irishmen movement – formed in Belfast in 1791 – these new radical ideas were spread around the countryside using popular broadsheets, pamphlets, and ballads. The United Irishmen, influenced especially by Wolfe Tone, sought to politicise the mass of the people and denounced attempts by the government to sectarianise Ireland. A Catholic priest from County Armagh, James O'Coigley, a member of the United Irishmen movement, made strenuous efforts in his native area of Armagh and Tyrone to persuade people to desist sectarian attacks. He was later arrested in London on his way to meet with Wolfe Tone in Paris, tried for treason, found guilty and hanged by the English authorities at Maidstone, Kent on 7 June 1798.[17]

With the attack on the official Catholic Church in France the Church authorities in Rome sought the support of the English monarch and government to defeat the revolution in France – before its 'atheistical' ideas spread any further.

Until then most Irish students for the priesthood were trained in Paris. They had been greatly disturbed by events taking place there; most were horrified with the way the French revolutionaries had treated the Catholic Church and clergy. Most had no difficulty in aligning with the English authorities and accepting instructions from Rome, warning of the dangers posed by the French republican ideas.

The Irish Catholic bishops had declared that it would be in the best interests of the Church if the training of priests could take place in their own country rather than in France, or anywhere else in Europe, where they might be influenced by new radical and anti-establishment ideas. Consequently, in 1795 the Irish bishops succeeded in obtaining a substantial financial grant from the English government for setting up and maintaining a Catholic seminary at Maynooth for the training of students for the priesthood in Ireland.

After Maynooth College was established, the Irish Catholic hierarchy was careful to show its support for government policy in the years preceding the 1798 rebellion. Bishops protested their loyalty to the crown and urged their priests and people to do likewise at every opportunity.

The United Irishmen were greatly influenced by ideas about democracy from France and America – and were encouraged by the prospect of armed help coming from France. The Catholic bishops saw this movement as a great threat to their new-found authority and to the status quo. The Irish bishops denounced the United Irishmen. The Rising planned for 1798 failed and the bishops promptly supported the British government's decision in 1800 to abolish the local Irish parliament and introduce an Act of Union by which Ireland would be ruled directly from Westminster. The bishops had hoped that the London government would reciprocate by granting the Catholics the right to sit in parliament (Catholic Emancipation). Due to local opposition as well as the intransigence of the Tories in England, this right was not conceded.

As the Irish Catholic middle class grew in numbers and confidence in the early 1800s it began to demand the right to be represented in the Westminster parliament. When the English parliament showed no willingness to grant this, the Catholic bishops and priests joined forces with Daniel O'Connell in his campaign, not for national freedom, but for Catholic middle-class emancipation and Catholic representation in parliament and the disestablishment of the Protestant Church. That recognition came in 1829 with the Catholic Emancipation Act. From then on well-off Catholics could sit in the English parliament. These reforms made no difference whatsoever in the lives of the vast majority of the population of eight million who were forced to live in poverty and who could not hope for even the right to be heard or any other concession from a Westminster parliament.

It has been argued that this all-Catholic movement for Catholic emancipation led by O'Connell and the clergy contributed a great deal to the growth of Protestant sectarianism in the north-east of the country. Protestant leaders like

Cooke and Hanna emerged to warn Protestants of the dangers and evils of Catholicism and 'popery'. The alliance of the Catholic hierarchy with progressive elements was short-lived. When O'Connell proceeded to organise for repeal of the Act of the Union the Irish bishops withdrew their support and resources. The movement flopped. The Young Ireland movement organised to carry on the resistance, culminating in the 1848 rebellion – which was confined to a few parishes.

Throughout this period – through the Great Hunger when the population was halved – the Catholic hierarchy consolidated its social standing in Irish society and became the accepted (ie, by the ever-increasing Irish middle class) leaders of the Catholic population in Ireland.

As its power increased and as it became more organised the Catholic Church became more authoritarian, more Roman and less Irish. The result was that a gap developed between people and clergy which increased as the struggle for political and cultural independence gained momentum. It was at this time that the Church became more formal; the custom of addressing priests as 'Father' was introduced and priests were compelled to wear the Roman collar.

There is little doubt that Archbishop Paul Cullen (1850-1878) was a most influential figure in bringing in the new practices; he carried out exactly the wishes of the Vatican for the Church in Ireland. He introduced new devotions and prayers from the Continent, eg, Forty Hours, novenas etc. However, politically, Cullen was merely following in the footsteps of O'Brien, Troy, Caulfield and other bishops before him. He denounced the Fenians and called for them to be excommunicated.

It was during Cullen's period as Archbishop of Dublin that the Catholic Church extended its control of the national education system – established and financed by the British government since 1831. That strategic move by the bishops (sanctioned at the Synod of Thurles in 1850) was to be the most significant development in the growth in power of the Catholic Church hierarchy and has lasted to the present day.

It was to the bishops that the English rulers looked for

support in times of popular rebellion in Ireland. The bishops, for the most part, did not disappoint the English with the vehemence of their condemnation of those who would dare rebel against 'the lawful government'. One MP stated in parliament, during the debate to increase the contribution to Maynooth College in the 1850s, that a loyal priesthood in Ireland was worth more than a standing army.[18]

The British government could rely on the bishops to run education in the best interests of the state. The Church was a conservative and anti-democratic institution.The Catholic hierarchy – with some notable exceptions – was quite happy with the status quo since the British government allowed them to have complete control over the schools. Incidentally, these schools contributed greatly to the demise of the Gaelic language since they promoted teaching through English. The hierarchy, with the notable exception of John McHale of Tuam, encouraged this. Canon Peadar Ó Laoire, in *Mo Scéal Féin*, wrote about the national school he attended:

> Most of the young people were learning Catechism through English, without one word of Gaelic ... I don't think that so great an injustice was ever done to young people's minds in any part of the world as was done to the youth of Ireland when this type of teaching was forced on them.[19]

Ó Laoire comments:

> The schools played a major part in the decline of the Irish language and in the growth of the national inferiority complex. Twenty years after the first schools were founded, although Irish was still spoken by more than one-fourth of the population, all lessons were given in English and very harsh measures were taken to discourage the use of the language among the children.[20]

During the last quarter of the nineteenth century the power of the Catholic clergy increased greatly. Even though many socially-committed priests were involved in the Land League movement, the Catholic Church establishment was regarded by some contemporary commentators as the real enemy of political and economic progress in the country. In his book, *Priests and People in Ireland* published in 1902, the Catholic barrister, John McCarthy, denounced the greed of the clergy and their control of the minds of the children as the single greatest evil in Irish society. McCarthy paints a most depressing picture and writes with a justifiable sense of outrage at what he witnessed on his travels around the country. He shows how the Catholic middle class was given special treatment by the clergy. For example in the Catholic Church in Lisbellaw, in County Fermanagh;

> I noticed that one of the open benches in the body of the Church had a red cushion on the seat, and another cushion on the kneeling stool. It was not the first bench next to the altar rails, but was in the second or third row. It struck me as peculiar and I avoided it. When I had been seated for some time, an elderly and a young lady in seal-skin jackets appeared and took possession of this cushioned seat.

McCarthy continues:

> Our priests profess to be no respecter of persons or wealth, but the truth is, that the greatest school for snobbishness and class distinction in the world is our Roman Catholic Church. It is always ready to grovel before the possessors of money, and to place freely at their disposal not only a soft seat and kneeling stool in the midst of bare discomfort, in return for their money, but also the sacramental treasures of the Church. Nowhere else are rich people – especially the young – so spoiled and flattered as they are by our priests and nuns. Our 'Church' often boasts that it is the Church of the poor, but it only deserves that title in the sense that it keeps the bulk of the members in poverty.[21]

The clergy throughout the country, according to McCarthy, were greedy, grasping and authoritarian. He accused them of 'spiritually bullying the poor'.

As the power and influence of the official Catholic Church increased so too did its arrogance and unwillingness to countenance any change in the political status quo. In all the attempts to overthrow the power of the landlords and the English in Ireland the official Church consistently took the side of the government and condemned those who resisted. In 1798, 1848, 1857, and the War of Independence, the Irish Catholic bishops condemned the leaders of the rebellion and excommunicated them. Even the non-military campaigns aimed at improving the lot of the people (eg, the Land League) were opposed and denounced by the Catholic hierarchy – with a few honourable exceptions. In adopting this policy the Churchmen were merely being obedient servants of the Vatican which, for its own political reasons, sought to cultivate good relations with the British government. The Irish hierarchy was also acting out of self-interest.

The development of a subservient hierarchical Church had a negative impact on the political and social development of a people who have been to this day controlled on the one hand by an outside government and on the other by a strong authoritarian Church.

In the years prior to the setting up of the 26 county state in 1922, the Catholic Church throughout the world after the First Vatican Council (1850-52) had become more autocratic and authoritarian. The experience in the USA, as described by theologian Rosemary Radford Reuther, is indicative of the trend at the time:

In the late nineteenth century progressive bishops such as John Ireland and intellectuals ... sought to articulate a new reconciliation of Catholicism to liberal values. These values included the separation of Church and state and religious pluralism, an active role for the laity in shaping the mission of the Church and the support of movements for social justice in the larger society, particularly the rights of labour. But these efforts were stifled by the Vatican condemnation of a vaguely defined heresy called 'Americanism' in 1897. Its full-scale death and burial followed the purges of any progressive ideas in American Catholic seminaries and colleges in response to the condemnation of modernism in 1907. These purges virtually destroyed nascent American Catholic intellectual life for a generation ... The American Church, which had a strong liberal tradition, was influenced by European Catholicism, centred in a triumphalistic papacy which felt that the answer to the Enlightenment was increased institutional monarchism and ideological infallibism. American democratic values were seen as a threat to authority in a Church in which authority was the essence of Catholicism. This identification of Catholicism with monolithic authoritarianism was expressed by a directive issued in 1907 that signalled the demise of earlier traditions of parish self-government:

The Church is not a republic or a democracy, but a monarchy ... all her authority is from above and rests in her Hierarchy; while the faithful of the laity ... have absolutely no right whatever to rule and govern.[22]

The official Church had adopted a similar approach in Ireland as the example of the Kilkenny-born priest, Walter MacDonald shows. MacDonald was a professor of Theology at St Patrick's College in Maynooth who had progressive ideas about the Church's role in Irish society:

MacDonald had the supreme audacity to suggest that the Catholic Church in Ireland should publish a detailed financial budget telling the people where their contributions went; and he said in 1908 that the Church should endorse the principle that the people had a right to control State-endowed schools: that if priests wished to retain their present position as sole managers they should do so as delegates of the people.[23]

These ideas were frowned upon by the authorities in Maynooth and the governing body, the bishops. Revolutionaries, whether engaged in an armed conflict or those like Fr Michael O'Flanagan who were urging fundamentally different economic and social structures were denounced and marginalised. Peadar O'Donnell, a leading republican activist, writer and intellectual suffered the fate of those who challenge the existing status quo. As a result of his opinions and his active involvement in campaigning on behalf of oppressed workers, he was ostracised and condemned by the leading figures in the political and religious establishment.

Nothing more clearly illustrates the paranoia and obsession of the Catholic clergy with social control than the Gralton case in County Leitrim in the 1920s and 1930s. Jimmy Gralton was a Leitrim man, born in 1886. He went to the US, joined the navy and became a US citizen. He had become a committed socialist. In 1921 he returned to his native County Leitrim to look after his aging parents on their small family farm. He tried to organise the local people.

The Black and Tans had burnt down the parochial hall in Gowel so there was no place for the young to meet. Gralton offered to build a hall on his father's farm with his own money – if the local people would provide voluntary labour. They built the hall beside Effernagh cross-roads and it was opened in 1921. It was called the Pearse/Connolly Hall. The Catholic clergy were furious:

> Fr McGaver of Kiltubrid condemned it and Gralton. He said he would put horns on him as he was an anti-Christ. Gralton went down to see Fr McGaver on hearing that. He knocked on the door and the housekeeper answered. He said he wanted to see Fr McGaver and he would pay him £5 if he would put the horns on him, as he would make an easier living in a circus if he had a pair of horns! He heard no more about it.[24]

His cousin Margaret Gralton continues:

> The clergy were furious, and started condemning dance-halls as occasions of sin from the altar in Gowel and Carrick-on-Shannon and they named the Pearse/Connolly Hall as one such place. Even before the hall was built they had warned people not to draw stones or sand to it, or their animals would be dead within the year, but the animals survived ... They were upset by the holding of classes in the hall: Gralton was usurping their authority. He was accused of indoctrinating the youth with socialist propaganda. Socialism, like sex, was a mortal sin in 1921.[25]

A land campaign was organised to have Wilton Waugh's huge estate in County Leitrim divided up among the locals. Gralton visited Waugh and told him what they intended to do. Within two weeks Gralton was arrested in Athlone. The locals protested and he was released after a week.

> Fr O'Reilly of Gowel was at this time denouncing Gralton off the altar. He brought in two Redemptorist priests, Fr Nolan and Fr Lawrence to hold a mission in Gowel in late May and early June. They could be heard down the road roaring about the anti-Christ in their midst and the dangers of socialism. They visited houses to warn parents to keep their children away from Pearse/Connolly Hall, and also warned them in confession that they would be refused absolution if they did not comply.[26]

Gralton was deported back to the USA in 1933 by the Fianna Fáil government under De Valera – one of the most shameful acts of the newly independent state. There was not a word of protest from the religious leaders.

In 1932 – the year of the Eucharistic Congress – as Jim Gralton was being expelled from Ireland, a Kilkenny man, Nixie Boran (1903-1971), was being condemned by the local bishop for his 'communistic views'. Boran and others had organised a union for the workers at the Castlecomer mines. He had also formed a study group 'The Revolutionary Workers Group' and a newspaper *The Workers Voice*. Bishop Collier of Ossory condemned all three undertakings.

> Soviet agents postured as labour leaders in an attempt to deceive the working class ... Agents would also pose as devout Catholics in furtherance of their objectives:
> They make it a point to be seen at Church, at Mass, at Devotions and then at the Sacraments. In Ireland this is one of their most dangerous weapons, and I know it has deceived and worried a good number of real Catholic workers. They say to the worker: I am a Communist but I am also a Catholic. I go to Church just as you do. Now to dispose of this subtle dishonesty for once and for all, I authoritatively say: No Catholic can be a Communist, no Communist can be a Catholic. For the formal professed Communist, any attendance at Church or sacraments is a mockery, a sacrilege, a profanation of holy things and must not lead people astray.[27]

Collier went on to denounce the local people:

> Wherefore it is my duty to tell my people plainly that the Revolutionary Workers Group, also all and every local union, cell or 'contact', which is communistic in aim and object has come under the ban and censure of the Church. No Catholic can be or remain a member of such a union, no matter what name they may adopt. Also, no Catholic can buy, sell, read, receive or support any Communistic literature, journal or paper such as *The Worker's Voice*.

One historian of this period concludes:

> It is certain that the virulent opposition from the Catholic clergy galvanised and hardened local opinion against the

union. The formidable power of the Catholic Church reigned supreme and it set the moral agenda. Drawn almost exclusively from the strong farmer class the clergy were socially conservative and intolerant of 'upstart' and 'ignorant' miners who dared to challenge the social orthodoxy. The founders of Boran's union were dismissed as 'a couple of cross-bred bainins from Clogh and a few half-idiots from Mooneenroe'. Neither were radicals such as Boran and his colleagues to reach any new Jerusalem in the new state. To people of no property like the miners the new state was little different to that which preceded it.[28]

The Irish Catholic Church continued to be authoritarian, defensive and inward looking, suspicious of democratic movements and afraid of local community initiatives it could not control. In the new 26 county state it became anti-intellectual and encouraged the censorship of a wide variety of writings. The 26 counties became a Catholic sectarian state. In Ireland since the 1920s women's rights have not been allowed to develop within the two conservative and male-dominated sectarian states.

The kind of Church that developed before and after partition is a far cry from the early Irish Church where priests and people worked together, where women were equal, where rules and regulations were secondary to looking after the needs of the people. The Church that emerged in the wake of the First Vatican Council and before the partition of Ireland was very much modelled on the Roman hierarchical Church – not the community or family Church based on the monasteries and the local communities that once existed in Ireland.

As the Church became more and more institutionalised the people handed over greater and greater responsibility to the institution. Church ruling replaced in great part the personal and conscience aspects of the faith ... In the long term institutionalisation devours the very thing on which it depends and feeds, namely the faith and personal and social commitment expressed by the people.[29]

Pope John XXIII in 1960 attempted to open the Catholic Church to the modern world and progressive influences.

84

The Second Vatican Council charted a new course for the universal Church. Sadly this new thinking has made little impact on the Irish Church – so ideologically reactionary, so entrenched politically, and so dominated by a conservative hierarchy.

The visit of Pope John Paul II to Ireland in 1979 confirmed the conservative view of the Church as 'the protector of the family' and 'defender' of the status quo. This has been further confirmed with the appointment of ultra-conservative bishops to Irish dioceses during his pontificate. Despite this, the late Cardinal Tomás Ó Fiaich tried, in his own way, to bring about a more open Church in Ireland. He was met with opposition or indifference from many of the other bishops.

During the hunger-strike of 1981 when Republican prisoners in the H-Blocks were demanding that the British government restore their status as political prisoners, the Irish hierarchy as a whole yet again demonstrated its policy of upholding the authority of the government with which it had become so closely aligned. As in the past, the hierarchy was acting out of perceived self-interest when it failed to intervene forcefully on behalf of the hunger-strikers and their supporters throughout the island. Instead of putting pressure on the government officials in London and Dublin to respond to the demands of the prisoners, the hierarchy put pressure on the hunger-strikers and their families to give up the protest.

***

There is a need to take a clear look at the kind of Church that has evolved in Ireland over the centuries and to look at the potential for a change in direction and pastoral practice in order to recover some of the native independence and spirituality of the early Celtic Church. If the Church fails to recover that richness it will continue to decline – in numbers, influence and credibility.

If the precious sensitivity and compassion of the Celtic faith is to be recovered, the Church must adopt a different pastoral approach – in favour of liberation rather than control. If the experience in Latin America is anything to go by, then this change must come from the people – the grassroots in small basic Christian communities organising throughout the whole country.

Resistance to the interference in Irish affairs by the English has been a feature of life in Ireland from 1170 to the present day. Indeed, Irish political history since then should properly be regarded as a history of resistance by the oppressed to British oppression. During certain periods when bishops and priests were targeted by the English authorities, the Catholic Church hierarchy was unavoidably involved in that resistance. At other times – and certainly in recent times, as the result of a deliberate policy by the British government of co-opting the Catholic hierarchy – it has tried to weaken that resistance.

The purpose of this overview of the history of the Irish Church is to show – from the point of view of the people who have been oppressed – how the official Church's role in Irish society has evolved and changed over the years according to its perceived interests. Too often this history has been written and presented from the point of view of the oppressors in order to discredit the struggle of the oppressed for justice and liberation.

Even from this cursory look at Irish Catholic Church history from the viewpoint of the oppressed, it becomes clear that the authoritarian anti-democratic Church which exists in Ireland today is not the kind of Church that has always existed in this country. Nor is this authoritarian Church the kind of Church that reflects all that is best in the Catholic tradition or in contemporary Catholic thinking and practice.

5

Challenging the Clerical Church

The priestly witness of Jesus was an announcement of abundance. His listeners were, like us, accustomed to the many barriers to and restrictions on God's abundance ... Religious institutions, then as now, made it their business to control and limit the believer's access to grace. But Jesus insisted that grace was everywhere, overflowing the official channels, available in astonishing abundance (James Whitehead, *Being a Priest Today,* [ed] Donald J Goergen).

If priestliness is about the abundance of grace, clericalism is about its scarcity (James Whitehead, *Being a Priest Today*).

It is more than 20 years since the Second Vatican Council (1961-65). That Council heralded a new era for the Catholic Church with the result that in some countries there have been radical changes in the Church's approach to social and political issues. But the Catholic Church in Ireland is still seen as a conservative reactionary organisation – politically and theologically. There is little room for open debate. The agenda of the official Church appears to be control – not liberation. The official Church does not address or confront the root causes of injustice and inequality in Ireland today.

The documents of the Council emphasise the priesthood of the laity and the Church as the People of God. This new emphasis was intended to counteract the clericalism that had grown up in the Church. The ordained ministers were to serve the priestly people, to help the people to recognise their priestly calling. The clerical Church is a denial of what Jesus preached about the role of religious leaders. As James Whitehead states so accurately: 'clericalism is neither identical with nor a necessary consequence of priesthood, but a diminishment and distortion of it'. Whitehead defines clericalism as 'the power to promote the particular interests of the clergy and to protect the privileges and power that have traditionally been conceded to those in the clerical state'.

This clerical attitude manifests itself in an authoritarian style of ministerial leadership, a rigidly hierarchical world view and a virtual identification of the holiness and grace of the whole Church with the clerical state. 'The laity often fall into clericalism when their contributions to the Church are made in an elitist or dominating fashion.'[1]

Clericalism then is to be challenged and opposed because it is limiting the role of the laity in the Church. The non-ordained are excluded from leadership. In this way, 'clericalism makes grace scarce'.[2] Laypersons are told they cannot preach; this makes the good news scarce. Ordination is restricted to unmarried men; this guarantees that the sacraments are in short supply. 'Only by letting go of the divisive categories of cleric and lay can we grasp again the energy and abundance of priestliness.'[3]

And, according to Whitehead:

> the most grievous offense of clericalism is its ambition to control the exuberant flow of the Spirit. While the priestly ministry of Jesus testifies to abundance clericalism restricts that grace.[4]

The effects of this clerical Church are to be seen in the Ireland of the 1990s. It is possible that by a common pastoral strategy to tackle the widespread poverty and inequality in Irish society a new Church might be born which respects the priestliness of all the baptised. It will demand courageous and wise leadership and a total commitment to real change. If Catholics are to have anything credible to say about democracy and equality in society then it is imperative that the Church itself is working to become a more democratic and just society. That is why the hierarchical Church needs to be balanced by the popular Church – and the two must be allowed to coexist – no matter how difficult and painful that may be for some.

There must grow within the Church in Ireland small groups of people committed above all to justice and equality.

They should demand that bishops and parish priests make the parish facilities available to them. It is a cause for concern to many to hear of priests refusing to allow certain groups to use parochial property because they do not like their politics.

As Whitehead correctly states:

> The priestly witness of Jesus testifies to abundance. Jesus' life proclaims an abundance of grace – wherever his followers act as a priestly people through their daily sacrifice of mercy, justice and love. The priestliness of the faithful does not rob the leader of his own – unless we are still embedded in a world of scarcity.[5]

While Irish Catholicism seems to be in a healthy enough state there are signs that not all is as well as it appears on the surface. Large numbers, especially of young people in the cities, have stopped going to Mass. Surveys show that a majority of Catholics no longer accept the Church's teaching on birth control. They also show that a growing segment does not support the Church's rigid stand on divorce.

While there is evidence also of dissatisfaction with the Church among the middle class – especially women – the most serious sign of a growing crisis is the alienation of a large section of the working class/unemployed from the institutional Church.

Faced with a situation of growing poverty and with the flagrant abuse of people's rights by those in power, censorship and the questionable tactics of police forces north and south, we must ask questions about the relevance of the clerical Church – and the effectiveness of a Church which adopts the hierarchical model to the exclusion of others. Where is the sense of anger and outrage characteristic of a genuine Christian response? Where is the determined action against the injustice and oppression – the daily violation of human rights by those in power?

The efforts of some religious groups like the Conference of Major Religious Superiors (CRMS) and the bishops in the west of Ireland to analyse the economic situation and highlight the bias against the poor are useful but limited. Insofar as the Religious Orders have attempted social analysis and have even gone to live and work alongside the poor, they have begun to show solidarity with the powerless rather than with the powerful and have pointed a way forward for the Church in Ireland.

At times in our history when the Church was prepared to stand with the people the official Church suffered and the bishops and priests were persecuted along with their people. At other times when the Church, taking its instructions from the Vatican, sought to strengthen its own organisation and control there was an accommodation with the political authorities. This accommodation continues to the present day. That alliance creates tension and division within the Catholic Church between those in Ireland who uphold the unjust status quo and those who oppose it.

The division within the Irish Catholic Church reflects the class division in society. Many among the clergy, who come mostly from the middle class, do not accept that there is real and systemic poverty and oppression in this country. Certainly the bishops have not analysed the political causes of the poverty and oppression.

The Catholic hierarchy set out to address the issue of justice in Ireland in a statement issued in 1977 without referring to the problems created by partition and British interference. The weakness of their approach to the deep-seated problems facing the Irish people is revealed in statements like these:

> We also exclude from consideration in this document many of the special questions of justice related to the violence in Northern Ireland ... Unemployed youth can very easily be attracted to the myths and deluded by the propaganda of the paramilitaries. Effective measures to reduce Northern Ireland's unemployment would, with guarantees against religious discrimination or paramilitary interference in the location of industries or the allocation of jobs and houses, make a real contribution to the prospects for peace.[6]

As in the case of unemployment it must be said that a systematic programme to eliminate poverty in Northern Ireland

90

would be likely to have a significant effect on violence in the so-called 'ghettos'.[7]

In another pastoral published in 1992 the Catholic bishops again fail to address the underlying political causes of poverty, unemployment and inequality.[8] There is in Ireland – in both states – real poverty in the midst of great wealth which is in the hands of a minority – some of whom live in a luxury comparable to anywhere in the world. In the southern 26 county state approximately 20% of the population own 80% of the wealth. In the north-eastern 6 county state approximately 15% of the people own 85% of the wealth. This inequality and injustice are such integral parts of the system that what we are dealing with is structural injustice – consolidated with the partitioning of this country.

Neither the Catholic Church hierarchy nor any of the peace and justice groups within the Catholic Church, eg the Irish Commission for Justice and Peace (ICJP) have identified or addressed the colonial causes of inequality and poverty in Ireland. That inequality has been institutionalised by the forced partition of the island by the British in 1920 enshrined in the Government of Ireland Act.

As a result many Catholics who belong to the poor and oppressed section of Irish society see the Church as irrelevant to their major concerns – unemployment and emigration and the growing gap between rich and poor throughout Ireland. They see the Church hierarchy's preoccupation with sexuality as imbalanced and disproportionate to concerns with social justice issues. With regard to the northern conflict, the obsession of some clerics with republican violence out of its historical and social context, and to the exclusion of institutional violence, must be regarded as political posturing.

The clerical Church is now more often criticised as being irrelevant to the basic needs of the vast majority of the Irish people – the right to dignified employment, the right to be heard and to have a voice; the right to be treated equally before the law. It is seen by many as an obstacle to the development of a pluralistic society.

91

There are some who see it as an obstacle to peace in the north because of the alignment of the hierarchy and clergy with the political establishment and the politically motivated refusal of the Church leaders to demand that the elected representatives of all the people be involved in any discussions about the future of the country.

The official Catholic hierarchy in Ireland has become identified with and is seen to be identified with the well-to-do middle class. The Catholic Church in Ireland has not clearly identified itself with the poor and the oppressed and their various struggles. It has not made a clear and convincing public analysis of the reasons for poverty. For that reason the poor and oppressed do not see the Church as acting in their interests or speaking on their behalf. Some are disillusioned and angry. Others could not care.

During the past 20 years of conflict in the north-east of Ireland the division within the Catholic Church along class lines has deepened. It is now the belief of many that in spite of the rhetoric about the unemployed and poor in places like West Belfast, the official Church is biased in favour of the rich and powerful. Its involvement in government-funded work schemes is interpreted as merely a ploy to maintain social control in certain areas and to try to marginalise support for republican parties which challenge the status quo.

An examination of the impact of the 1981 hunger-strike makes it obvious that this bias in favour of the establishment is not just confined to the Church leaders in the north of Ireland but is the attitude of the official Catholic Church throughout the whole country. When a leading Catholic cleric states that the Catholic middle class should provide the real political leaders, we see the unambiguous bias of the Church in favour of a particular class. That bias has developed over the years especially since the mid-1800s when the Church took over the running of the schools.

In the context of the conflict in the north of Ireland the official Church has shown by its silence about police torture and harassment that it supports the powerful against the weak. That support is purely pragmatic – in order to preserve its own power and ability to control and to ensure financial support from the government. There is poverty and hardship – caused by years of neglect by the government. The Churchmen do not address this form of violence. The poor are harassed and abused every day by some arm of the government and yet the Church leaders remain silent.

The Church has taken the wrong side – the side of the status quo – in order to maintain power and control. It has opposed the people's struggle for human rights, justice and freedom – in stronger terms than the British government. This is not because it feels any bond with the government but because it feels its own power and control threatened by those who seek the overthrow of British power and the end of partition.

The British government sees the Catholic hierarchy in Ireland as a significant social power which cannot be ignored if it hopes to maintain control in Ireland. As part of the strategy for pacifying Ireland it has decided today, as in the past, to use the Catholic Church as an instrument of its own political policy. While the Catholic Church does not have the power and influence that it did in the past, the British government still sees it as an important bulwark to stop the drift towards independence and republicanism.

They realise that the support of the Catholic hierarchy is absolutely necessary if they are to put into effect their primary political aim in the north of Ireland – stabilisation. Stability is the aim of the British government in Ireland. We have a situation where two powerful forces which have nothing in common – except social control – co-operate to maintain that control.

In the south the official Catholic Church has traditionally supported and maintained the status quo and finds itself in an even stronger situation. The bishops have not made a clear analysis of the real reasons for the poverty and unemployment which plague the 26 counties. To do so would raise too many political implications and contradictions for the Church itself. Some more liberal bishops make statements from time to time about these issues – but statements are clearly not enough to effect a change in government policy.

93

However, even though it still maintains control over the education of Catholics, the Catholic Church is losing its influence and its moral authority especially in the context of the development of republican and socialist politics. Many Catholics have already walked away, some try to build a loyal opposition. The 'silent majority' drift along without really thinking too seriously about the situation or else are afraid to risk any kind of confrontation with the clergy or hierarchy.

It is not likely that the Catholic people throughout Ireland will jettison their long history of popular faith and devotion overnight. But the signs are, especially among the young in the larger urban areas, that many are already leaving the institutional Church because they feel it does not meet their needs or represent their interests. It is seen as dominated by the clergy. It has become identified with the political and social establishment. The institutional Catholic Church still has support but increasingly, as far as the poor are concerned, it is remote and preaches an irrelevant message.

Is the Catholic Church now prepared to return to its roots and take the risk of annoying the powerful by identifying with the poor? Is it prepared to put its own house in order, to pay its own workers and make available its resources to the poor?

What is needed is an honest critique of the past and an open admission that the Catholic Church has made mistakes and has taken the wrong side by supporting the unjust status quo. A new approach is called for if the Church is to address the deep social, political and economic problems facing the people. A new theology must begin with an analysis of the political and social reality, followed by theological reflection, followed by pastoral considerations.

In Ireland, certainly at the official level, the understanding of the faith has been influenced greatly by the most orthodox European writers and scholars most of whom pursued a conservative theology which upheld at all costs the official governments and rulers. It has been uncritical of an unjust political status quo and encourages blind loyalty to those in power.

That theology is still the prevailing theology within the clerically dominated Irish Catholic Church today. It is for the most part abstract and unrelated to the specific needs and problems of the people living here today. As James Cone, the African American theologian, writes about the similar situation facing the African American Church:

> I contend that when theological discourse overlooks the oppressed and the hope given by Jesus Christ in their struggle, it inevitably becomes abstract talk, geared to the ideological justification of the status quo.[9]

In Ireland where the vast majority of the population belongs to the Catholic Church – in the sense that it is where they are baptised and buried – it is important to look at how Catholics have been taught to understand their Christian faith and how they are involved in the life and mission of the Church. It is necessary to look again at the political and social context in which Jesus and the early disciples lived and especially at the reasons for Jesus' arrest, and crucifixion. Without understanding this essential part of Jesus' life and message we will not accept the limitations and weaknesses of conventional theology nor accept the urgent need for a liberation theology in this country.

The Catholic Church in Ireland has not assimilated the theology of the Second Vatican Council which stressed the priesthood of all the baptised. It has adopted the liturgical changes insofar as they affect the architecture of the churches and the minimal involvement of laity as readers, ministers of the Eucharist etc, but there is no discussion of the meaning and demands of the Christian faith in a situation where there is severe poverty, unemployment, discrimination and harassment.

The alliance of Church and state allows the Catholic bishops to continue in their role as upholders of the social system. After all, the British government provides financial support for Catholic education. The bishops do not appear to be prepared to jeopardise this kind of money by confronting the government. They do not appear to be prepared to bite the hand that feeds them.

But they now must answer to those members of the Church who say that neither social control nor support for the social system is part of their mission. It has no basis in the Gospel or the Church's teaching. It is an aberration which has become part of the Church's policy.

In contrast according to liberation theology it is precisely this issue that must be discussed – the relationship of Church and state and how that relationship affects the lives of the poorest of the poor. Liberation theology raises many questions about the traditional political alignments of the Church as well as the exercise of power within the Church itself.

6

Partition and Poverty

*Poverty is not only about shortage of money. It is about rights and
relationships; about how people are treated and how they regard
themselves; about powerlessness, exclusion and loss of dignity. Yet the
lack of an adequate income is at its heart* (Carey Oppenheim, *Poverty,
the Facts*).

*A series of new geographical boundaries has come to divide the UK,
marking off the affluent regions and countries from the poorest. Northern
Ireland ranks as the poorest on all counts – unemployment, poverty and
low incomes* (Carey Oppenheim, *Poverty, the Facts*).

Research shows that in the south of Ireland (26 counties)
31.4% of the population live below the poverty line; 40% of
children in the south live in poverty. In the 6 counties 27% of
the total population and 36% of children live in poverty
according to the 1990 Report of the Child Action Group.

What is poverty? Homeless people? pensioners in
hovels? travellers begging on the streets? single parent families trying to manage on supplementary welfare payments?
It is not easy to define poverty though we see the results of
it. Furthermore, poverty differs from country to country and
from place to place. Poverty in Belfast or Cork is different
from poverty in Somalia and Ethiopia. But for those who are
poor the experience of humiliation and degradation is the
same anywhere.

There are three broad categories of poverty; absolute
poverty, relative poverty and a social consensus view of
poverty. Absolute poverty implies the absence of basic
physical needs – food, water, clothing, shelter, rather than
broader social and cultural needs. 'Absolute poverty is when
people cannot house, clothe or feed themselves.'[1] But there

are other forms of poverty – just as real and just as destructive of human beings.

Relative poverty is a term which describes the situation of those 'who lack the resources to obtain the type of diet, participate in the activities and have the living conditions and amenities which are customary or at least widely encouraged or approved, in the societies in which they belong.'[2]

Thus as Oppenheimer states:

> Poverty is not simply about lack of money but also about exclusion from the customs of society. Relative poverty is about social exclusion imposed by inadequate income. It is not only about having to go short of food or clothing. It is also about not being able to join a local sports club, or send your children on a school trip, or go out with friends, or have a Christmas dinner.[3]

There is a third form of poverty called the 'consensual view' in which social consensus about poverty is used as a guide. Poverty was defined in relation to the standard of living of a particular society.

> People should have the right to an income which allows them to participate in society rather than merely exist.[4]

The poverty we are talking about in relation to Ireland belongs mostly to the second and third categories. Statistics are only a small help towards understanding the reality of poverty. It has to be experienced in order to be properly understood. But statistics can give us an indication of the extent of the problem.

At least 40% of the population of the island of Ireland is estimated, according to standards defined by the EC, to live below the poverty line. There is an enormous gap between the 'haves' and the 'have-nots'. In the 26 counties, 20% of households own virtually nothing in terms of assets (ie, land, homes, bank accounts, shares in stock, etc). The wealthiest 10% of households – the majority of whom are large farmers, managers, top professionals – own nearly 50% of all the personal wealth in the 26 counties. In contrast the poorest 50%

98

(or half the population) own only 12% of all the wealth. It is estimated, in a recent survey, that the wealthiest 1-2% of all the households own up to 30% of all wealth.[5]

This disparity carries over into the political, social, economic and legal structures. In Ireland, as elsewhere, wealth equals influence and the wealth of this country is controlled by a very small percentage of wealthy elites. Thus the majority of the Irish people are rendered powerless and voiceless.

Some claim that poverty is caused by the weather or by laziness or by the world recession; and that violence is caused by people who have nothing better to do and who are intrinsically evil. They never seem to think that there might be other reasons for poverty and violence in Irish society.

Because of the superficial and banal explanations for poverty and violence, we need social analysis in order to identify the root cause of inequality and poverty in our country. With social analysis we find that the causes are deeply rooted in the economic and political system – a system which was devised and institutionalised, when Ireland was partitioned, to benefit some at the expense of others and preserve, at all costs, the stability of an unjust arrangement.

In the north of Ireland (6 counties) the unemployment rate according to the Department of Economic Development (DED) is 14% of the workforce. However, a series of statistical manipulations by the government (eg adding people on schemes to the workforce) gives a misleading impression of the employment rate. In the south of Ireland (26 counties) 19% of the labour force is unemployed and here also training schemes are needed to take many off the unemployment register. Not only has the target for the number of jobs failed to emerge – both north and south – but those few new jobs which have been created are generally badly paid and insecure.

Figures published for emigration from the 6 counties are for 1983, when 4,360 left, and 1990, when 7,200 are reported to have emigrated.[6] It is estimated that more than 6,000 working age people have left each year since 1983. The total number of emigrants from the north from 1982-1990 is in the region of 50,000. This is only an approximate estimate and the real number is surely much higher. In the 26 counties between 1980 and 1989, 250,000 people emigrated. Most of these were forced to emigrate by economic circumstances. At present (1992) more than 265,000 people (19% of the workforce) are unemployed and this number is set to top 300,000.

This failure of current economic strategy has been recognised by the Conference of Major Religious Superiors (CMRS) in their response to the 1990 Budget in the 26 counties when they stated:

> The (Dublin) government's strategy for eliminating poverty has focused mostly on job creation. However, these jobs are not materialising, nor is there any likelihood that they will be created in the foreseeable future on anywhere near the scale required to eliminate poverty. Consequently change was urgently needed. Otherwise the gap between the poor and the rest of society would continue to widen and we would see Ireland locked into a deeply divided two-tier society.[7]

There have been many commentaries about Ireland's economic 'troubles' – high unemployment, emigration, growing income inequality and widespread poverty. Seldom is attention given to the root cause of these ills.

A major cause of Ireland's relative economic under-development and poverty lies in partition and the consequent denial of the Irish people's right to democratic control over their own economy. We need to examine how partition has significantly contributed to the relative under-development and the subsequent poverty, discrimination, emigration and overall misery experienced by a vast number of people on the island.

Historically, the British colonisation of Ireland distorted its economic development. (As in Africa and Asia, the Irish economy existed merely to service the needs of Britain.) During the eighteenth and nineteenth centuries the foundations for partition were being laid. Ireland's economy was a classic case of imperial feudalism: large land holdings owned by absentee British landlords and worked by peasant tenant farmers whose output was exported to Britain.

Industry had grown in the northern part of the island

because of the different land tenure system which existed in Ulster. The bulk of the people outside of Ulster were tenants-at-will but in Ulster tenant rights (which resulted from legislation developed during the plantation period – to make Ireland attractive to settlers from Britain) existed. The land system made productive investment in the south of Ireland impossible. 'Tenant rights' in Ulster allowed security of tenure and led to an increase in the value of land. By the end of the eighteenth century, with the exception of Guinness breweries, industry in the south had virtually disappeared despite the fact that at the beginning of the eighteenth century it had been more developed than in the north.

During the 1830s the suffering of the Irish peasantry continued as Westminster forced an Irish Poor Law through in 1838. In 1845, the Devon Commission estimated that £7 million poured out of Ireland annually to absentee landlords. In 1845 a blight of the Irish potato crop – the basic food of the peasants (and workers) – meant starvation for a large section of the population.

During the years of the Great Hunger (1845-1849) Ireland's population fell from over eight million to four million. During the first three months of the Great Hunger, 258,000 quarters of grain, 701,000 hundredweights of barley and 1 million quarters of oats and oatmeal were exported out of Ireland into England at a profit while over one million people died of starvation. After that date, exports continued at the same rate, producing profits for landlords, a cheap source of agricultural commodities which assisted Britain in her pursuit of rapid industrialisation, and resulting in death and starvation for Irish peasants.

Prior to 1920, colonialism continued to impede Ireland's economic development leading to periodic starvation, unequal distribution of land and a very limited industrial base in only one area of the entire country – the area around Belfast. That industrial base consisted of two industries: shipbuilding and textiles (mostly linen). This dependence on a very limited number of industries set the 6 counties up for its inevitable economic crisis and left the 26 counties with no industrial base at all before 1920. (The industries that were developed in and around Belfast directly served Britain's imperial and war interests – ships, low cost clothing and military uniforms etc.)

The British government's economic and political interests – and not the alleged allegiance to loyalists – clearly lay behind the decision to partition Ireland. The English believed that, given the north's industrial base, it would, like their other colonies at the time, provide a healthy surplus. Indeed up until 1927 the north actually had a surplus and paid England an 'imperial tax'. There was no reason for England to expect that this contribution to its treasury would not continue in the future.

However Britain failed to recognise that partition would hinder the development of an island economy such as that of Ireland. The partition of the nation severely reduced the economies of scale which could be realised by industries in Ireland.

Economies of scale are usually considered, along with a well-planned and developed infrastructure, to be an essential ingredient for achieving industrial competitiveness, especially during the early stages of a nation's development. The reason for this is that the economies of scale can enable an economy to obtain the 'critical mass' required for it to reach the stage of economic development known as 'the take-off period' where industries become competitive in world markets and the nation experiences rapid economic development – eg, Japan in the late 1970s. Partition forever hinders Ireland's 'take-off'.

During the 1950s when it became clear that Ireland was failing to develop, politicians and development agencies, instead of challenging and acknowledging that partition was a key reason for this, embarked upon a policy of wooing foreign investors. These were – and still are – offered large financial incentives to locate in Ireland. Again due to partition the development agencies in the north (IDB) and in the south (IDA) often find themselves competing for the same multinational company.

The pattern of multi-national expansion in Ireland is typical of world practice. Foreign investors establish branch factories in the 'host' country where assembly is the primary activity. Research and development are almost completely lacking. Foreign investors receive huge financial incentives plus the added benefit of relatively low wages which allows them to obtain very high rates of profit (10% of GDP in the 26 counties leaves Ireland as foreign investors appropriate their profits out of Ireland). They remain in Ireland until the incentives are withdrawn or reduced or until workers demand high wages and/or better working conditions. Then the multi-national goes off to some other developing country whose government thinks this kind of foreign investment is the panacea for economic development.

Alongside this bureaucracy is the fact that US, German, British and Japanese multi-nationals take billions in profits out of the country. In 1989, 6 billion pounds left the country in capital flight to multi-national profits and foreign investments. This is allowed because of the laws in the 26 counties which have reduced the taxation on multi-nationals to between 0-9% per annum – the lowest corporate tax in Europe. The next lowest is Italy at 36%. All the other EC countries have corporate tax rates over 40%. Because of this the burden of taxation in the 26 counties has shifted to the individual worker.

Foreign investment has never developed any nation – not in Latin America, Africa and certainly not in Ireland. Contrary to popular rhetoric (espoused by both the British and Irish governments) foreign investment does not inevitably lead to economic development and, therefore, does not reduce unemployment and poverty.

The Irish agriculture and food industry has failed to develop its full potential as a result of the partition of this small country. Since partition, the 26 counties continued to export cattle and grain mostly to Britain where prices were poor. When the south joined the EEC (now EC) in 1972 there was a larger market for agricultural produce and prices increased.

However, in spite of claims about the benefits of the EC to Irish farmers – north and south – it must be stated that it has benefited only some from the farming community –

those individuals who own large farms and those engaged in intensive crop, dairy or livestock farming. It has been disastrous for the small farmers, forcing most to go on the dole or to emigrate. It must be remembered that the vast majority of the farmers in the west of the country lived on small holdings.

If the small farmers are to survive it can only be done through collective co-operative action. This is not encouraged at all in the north and not very successfully in the south. Due to the large economies of scale at work in agriculture as well as the large capital requirements involved in food processing, this collective action needs to pull together the resources of small farmers north and south. Partition hinders this. If programmes for rural self-help are to be efficient and feasible they must take place in an all-Ireland context.

The attempts to turn Ireland – north and south – into a tourist mecca must be questioned. According to some economists targeting tourism as a major industry is now thought to be damaging to tourism in the longer term.

In the 6 counties discrimination – apart from its moral and human rights considerations – has contributed to industrial inefficiency. This inefficiency is the result of workers not being matched to jobs based on their productive potential but rather on their religious affiliation.

Manufacturing productivity in the 6 counties is, on average, 20% lower than in Britain despite the massive subsidies that firms receive from the British government. Since most industrial jobs, especially high wage skilled ones, have been open to only one segment of the population – unionist males – the pool of applicants from which employers choose is highly limited. As a result the workforce is less trained, less productive and less motivated than if employment opportunities were open to all segments of the labour force. Obviously this has detrimental effects on the north's industrial productivity.

Naturally, discrimination results in a very uneven distribution of income in the 6 counties. The lowest 50% of the population receive 6% of the household income (earn 18% of the income) in the 6 counties. The top 10% earn 30% of all the income while the top 50% earn 82% of all the income (*cf* Family Earnings Survey 1981).

Income distribution in the 26 counties is just as bad if not worse – due to unequal distribution of wealth (ie, land holdings, etc) as well as a highly regressive system of taxation.[8] This means that the wealthy and especially the multinationals have a lower relative burden of taxation than those in middle and lower income tax brackets. Income inequality has serious consequences for economic development.

The 1989 pre-budget submission from the CMRS claimed that in the 26 counties 'there are more people living in poverty today than in the past 20 years. We are producing a deeply divided two-tier society of "haves" and "have-nots"'.[9] Their report highlights the fact that injustice in the south is a structural issue.

The effects of poverty are to be seen in the large housing complexes in the main cities and towns throughout the country. Poverty is seen in the overcrowded housing conditions, in the camp-sites of the travelling people, in the deprivation of social and recreational facilities for the people. This especially affects young people and the elderly.

> One of the clearest findings of research into poverty in the Irish Republic in the 1980s has been that, the longer the decade progressed, the more likely it became that the face of a person who was poor was that of a child, and that this poverty was due to unemployment ... The social welfare system coped least well with the challenge of supporting families where the joblessness of the head of the household persisted. In Ireland, north and south, society strongly values the family. One wonders, however, if we have really appreciated the enormous damage to family life wreaked by unemployment in the 1980s.[10]

One of the aims of any genuine democracy is to promote the well-being and welfare of all the citizens without fear of favour. It should also provide for the basic needs of all the citizens and ensure that the weakest and most vulnerable are allowed to play their full part in the social and economic life of the community. If equality of opportunity is to be protected and if meaningful employment is to be provided then economic activity should create wealth as well as gainful employment. Work schemes, such as Action for Community Employment (ACE) do not create wealth nor permanent employment.

In order to ensure the proper distribution of wealth in this country there needs to be a new strategy which seeks to create democratic structures and constitutional guarantees. The existing situation of a partitioned island economy with a colonial state in the north-east and a neo-colonial state in the 26 counties has led to corruption and inequality in both states. Partition has resulted in the militarisation of the 6 counties and especially the border region where the closing of roads by British authorities has resulted in the destruction of the economic and social life of these areas.

The reality of high unemployment and mass emigration in both states calls for a new approach to partition and the militarisation of the north by all concerned about the well-being and welfare of the people of this island. The existence in the 26 counties of a two-tier society which favours those who can easily afford private health care and education calls for a new approach to the political establishment in the south by the official Church which has acquiesced in this unchristian situation for too long.

Poverty and lack of jobs puts tremendous strains on family life. In households where the adults cannot get a job the situation is often made worse by alcohol abuse. Poverty worsens from generation to generation as the demoralisation and sense of hopelessness grows.

The only way to end the vicious cycle of poverty, unemployment and emigration in Ireland is through radical political reform which would result in an efficient economy with maximum employment in a wide range of jobs and a fair distribution of wealth. Partition prevents the development of a strong and vibrant economy in Ireland and without that jobs cannot be created. Catholic bishops, as moral leaders, have a grave responsibility not only to highlight the plight of the poor but to challenge those structures and institutions – starting with partition – that cause poverty and inequality.

The official Catholic Church may argue as it once did in

South Africa and in El Salvador that it should not get involved in politics. But the official Church is already involved in politics in supporting the status quo even though it may issue statements about unemployment and poverty which might appear to be critical of government.

The official Church, through the bishops, is obliged by the Gospels to bring about a real change in political attitudes and policies. The Catholic hierarchy can confront a basic cause of poverty and violence in Ireland by challenging the London government about its repressive and divisive policies in Ireland and by challenging the existing status quo in the south which accepts partition and inequality. The denial of national self-determination will continue to hinder economic development in Ireland.

A political solution is required which accepts that a unified country would not only be more in accordance with the principles of democracy but would also be a step in breaking the vicious cycle of poverty and dependency in Irish society. That would benefit all the inhabitants of Ireland. For that reason partition must become a primary moral issue for the Catholic Church.

Only in the context of national self-determination and the ending of partition will Ireland be able, as an independent and sovereign nation, to develop its economy by pooling and coordinating its resources simultaneously for the full benefit of all the Irish people.

Ireland has sufficient resources that nobody on this island should live in need. It has a highly educated, young population, capable of running an efficient, industrial, modern democracy. However, this efficient and equitable economy has failed to emerge. It has never been allowed or encouraged to develop.

The official Catholic Church – in Ireland and internationally – should be working for the creation of a democracy in Ireland. That means economic democracy – the only guarantee of justice. That will necessarily involve the Church leaders in a campaign to end partition – just as the Church leaders in South Africa are campaigning to end Apartheid. Both systems have similar economic consequences – poverty and systematic inequality. Both are based on privilege and both are morally evil.

It is now time for the official Catholic Church to examine its role in supporting the status quo including partition. That system of partition in Ireland is the root cause of poverty and inequality in this country. It is at the basis of the on-going conflict in our country and until it is dismantled there will not be peace.

7

Institutional Violence

Rather than being a liberal democratic society Northern Ireland is more akin to a military bureaucratic dictatorship ... From its very inception it has been impossible to govern Northern Ireland without the use of the most draconian emergency legislation. Trapped within its boundaries a large minority suffering oppression and discrimination refuse to accept their lot and have used a wide range of methods to free themselves (Robert Heatley, *Breaking the Deadlock*).

The peace in which we believe is, however, the fruit of justice. As a simple analysis of our structures shows and as history confirms, violent conflicts will not disappear until the underlying causes disappear ... We, therefore, regard as the most urgent task the establishment of social justice (*Archbishop Oscar Romero*, Third Pastoral Letter, 6 August 1978).

The partition of Ireland in 1921 was imposed by the British government against the democratic wishes of the majority of the Irish people. The statelet of Northern Ireland, consisting of the 6 north-eastern counties was formed on the basis of a religious headcount of the population. This was to ensure that the British would continue to control the political and economic life of the island through a permanent privileged and loyal majority. As a consequence of this undemocratic arrangement the nationalist/Catholic population of the 6 north-eastern counties was to be permanently excluded from power – through a systematic policy of gerrymander and discrimination. In itself, therefore, Northern Ireland is an inherently violent statelet which has encouraged structured discrimination and sectarianism since its foundation

The Irish Catholic bishops were, at first, critical of the partition of Ireland but later accepted it as a *fait accompli*. The Catholic bishops made their peace with the status quo and continued this co-operation with the British administration in the north as soon as they were assured of funding for Catholic schools and a Catholic hospital.

Meanwhile, many in their congregations were being murdered and attacked by those who saw Catholics as a threat to the state. The bishops, for the most part, were silent about this persecution of their own people. They remained silent about the fundamental reasons for the ongoing violence. With few exceptions they remained silent about the injustice and the discrimination. Throughout the 50 years of one party rule from Stormont the Irish Catholic hierarchy had nothing to say about the denial of the legal, civil and political rights of their own people. One of the northern bishops, Dr Mageean of Down and Connor, was extremely critical of the Stormont regime but did not have the public support of the other members of the Irish Bishops Conference which would have been necessary to make any impact on the political situation.

The Irish Catholic hierarchy has consistently supported the status quo because it believes that its power, and the status of the Church, as it understands it, is best guaranteed under the present system – especially since it receives British government funding for schools and colleges.

When Pope John Paul II visited Ireland in 1979, he commented on the conflict in the north, repeating the official line of the Irish Catholic hierarchy since 1970. All of their statements and pastorals relating to the north have consistently attacked the republican movement and warned people of the dangers of republicanism. Criticism of the British government has been as muted as it has been rare. Loyalist violence is seldom referred to – except in the context of blaming republicans for its very existence. In short, the target of Church condemnation has invariably been the IRA and the Sinn Féin party which espouses a republican position.

What the Pope's statement at Drogheda and virtually all official Church pronouncements have in common is their unwillingness to challenge the structural or institutional violence in Ireland. They have failed to recognise that republican violence is merely symptomatic of the underlying violence of partition and the institutionalised violence of the 6 county statelet.

In previous republican campaigns against the British in Ireland the Catholic hierarchy excommunicated the IRA. There are those who say it ought to be done again in order to distance the Catholic Church from republicans. Some bishops claim that the IRA excommunicate themselves. Catholic bishops seem to make the assumption that all republicans are Catholics. While it may be true to assume that a large percentage belong to the Catholic Church, it is quite erroneous to think of the IRA or any other republican grouping as a Catholic organisation.

Neither appeals from the Pope, the cardinals, the bishops nor the threat of excommunication have done anything to force the Catholics within the IRA to give up their military campaign. Is it not time, after more than twenty years of strife, that the leaders of the Catholic Church looked a little further to understand the reasons for the ongoing violent campaign? What is it that sustains this campaign? Why do young men and women join in a revolutionary organisation – when they will almost certainly end up either serving a long sentence in jail or else dead? These are the questions that those who moralise about violence need to ask in order to find a way forward – a way of resolving the conflict through a process of negotiation and dialogue.

If the Catholic hierarchy are to make any progress in their understanding of the situation and make any positive contribution to a resolution of the conflict they must examine the reasons for the existence of the IRA. They must define violence and analyse the causes of violence in our society. As Flann Campbell writes:

> There can be no long-term solution to the 'Ulster problem' until the true picture, warts and all if necessary, is shown. There can be no healing process until the real nature of the disease is carefully examined and its underlying pathology exposed and dealt with. In other words there can be no understanding of the present without a much fuller knowledge of the past.[1]

The denial of basic human and civil rights for almost fifty years of unionist rule in Northern Ireland led to the movement for civil rights in 1968. This is how another writer belonging to the Dissenter, ie, radical Protestant tradition, describes the Northern Ireland state:

> Northern Ireland as part of the British state in Ireland was not created by Irish democracy – Catholic or Protestant. Sir Edward Carson, leader of the Unionists did not devise Partition. He accepted it unwillingly ... Northern Unionists and Northern Nationalists were coerced or beguiled into a framework in which perpetual friction would be inevitable ... At the time the arrangement under the Government of Ireland Act 1920 was seen on both sides to this conflict as something of a stop-gap. No one was convinced of it as a permanent arrangement. One look at the contours of how the border was drawn is graphic proof of that. This gerrymander was the original anti-democratic act.[2]

As a result of the violent response of the right-wing unionists during 1968-71, some who had been involved in the IRA in the 1950s and early 1960s began to regroup to act as defenders of the Catholic people. At that time, they gained widespread acceptance from the Catholic clergy. The attacks during 1968-69 on Catholic homes in Belfast by police and loyalists and the killing of 14 civilian protesters in Derry on Bloody Sunday 1972 by British paratroopers led to the reorganisation of the IRA as an armed revolutionary organisation committed to war against the state and the British government. Its stated goal was, and remains, to force the British government to declare its intention of withdrawing from Ireland.

The IRA guerrilla campaign against the British government and the northern state has continued for over 20 years and shows little sign of going away. The IRA has a substantial degree of active and tacit support from within the nationalist community in spite of every possible attempt to undermine that support. Their support has remained solid mainly because a substantial percentage (30-40%) of the nationalist/Catholic population regard the political system in the 6 counties as hostile to them and their interests. That is their everyday experience. Their greatest suspicions and fears about what the British are doing in Ireland are confirmed when they hear of cases like that of the British agent, Brian Nelson,[3] who was responsible for the assassination of a number of Catholics.

As far as those who are active in or who support the republican campaign are concerned the way to secure peace is through a British declaration of intent to withdraw from Ireland and the creation of a democratic system of government for the whole country. Many would prefer to see this achieved by non-violent means but in the absence of any effective political alternative accept the inevitability of armed struggle.

In some Latin American countries Catholic Church leaders have not allowed media intimidation to deter them from giving support to the people's struggles for justice and liberation. That approach is not shared by the Irish Catholic hierarchy. Irish bishops have constantly issued condemnations of republicans – rarely of the government which is responsible for this conflict. They have no problem with meeting with British government ministers, representatives and civil servants as well as police (RUC) and army chiefs to discuss 'the security situation' and other political matters. At the same time, they refuse to conduct dialogue with the elected representatives of a large segment of the oppressed community. The bishops require them, but not the British and their allies, to renounce the physical force option.

The official Catholic Church in Ireland has, since O'Connell, supported constitutional nationalism. In the 6 counties Catholic priests in the 1940s and 1950s often acted as chairmen of the nationalist party branches. It was inevitable that most Catholic clergy could find the SDLP, which replaced the Nationalist party, an acceptable alternative to the growing radical political groupings that emerged with the civil rights campaign and the prison struggles. Certainly, some bishops and priests made no secret of their support for the SDLP. Many parish priests became active promoters of the party in their parishes – often simply by preaching from the pulpit about the evils of republicanism. Sinn Féin,

113

because of its commitment to securing a non-sectarian, egalitarian society, is seen as threatening the special position of the Catholic Church in Ireland.

The SDLP, which is supported by the Dublin and Washington political establishment has wide appeal among the Catholic middle-class, businessmen and professionals – who have been doing quite well economically throughout the 1970s and 1980s. For, while in the past, almost the entire nationalist/Catholic community had been subjected to discrimination and inequality and few could make it in the professional or business world, since the Civil Rights Movement the British government has ensured that a slightly larger section of the compliant and anti-republican Catholic population has now been allowed a greater share in the jobs and wealth of the state. They are the people who support the SDLP financially and who are also seen as 'the respectable' people in the Catholic Church. This professional Catholic middle class in the north is quite happy with the status quo.

While the British government's policy of anti-Catholic job discrimination still continues, it now affects the poorer section of the Catholic community more sharply than the Catholic middle class. Sinn Féin, as a political party, tends to receive most of its support from the most oppressed section of the Catholic community in the north – since that party clearly identifies the source of the poverty and the oppression experienced by the majority of the people living there. (Sinn Féin does not receive a similar degree of support in the 26 counties because the people in the south do not see that it is as relevant to their immediate needs. It is also hindered by the censorship of its views.)

The reality of the unjust political and economic situation in the north is not seen as an urgent issue by the Catholic middle class politicians, north and south – nor by the Catholic Church hierarchy. However, anti-Catholic discrimination goes to the heart of the conflict in the north. The real causes of the conflict must be recognised and dealt with if there is ever going to be a lasting peace. Catholic Church leaders could play an important role in identifying the *root causes* of the conflict. They could help to bring this conflict to an end by insisting that partition/the Government of Ireland Act and its dire economic and social consequences be on the agenda of any future political discussions. In adopting this policy, they would help to counter the appalling ignorance and prejudices of southern politicians and commentators like Garret Fitzgerald, Bruton, O'Brien, et al.

However, given the traditional hostility to movements for a national democracy in Ireland it seems unlikely that the Catholic bishops, as a group, will voluntarily change their pro-establishment policy. Only a well-organised movement at grassroots level within the Catholic Church in Ireland challenging the Catholic practice of opposing democracy and ignoring partition can bring about this change in direction.

The close political alignment of the Irish Catholic Church and the Vatican with the British government was obvious in the Pope's speech at Drogheda during his visit to Ireland in 1979. In 1991, when the Pope received a British ambassador to the Vatican, he once again ignored Britain's malign role in Ireland.[4]

The Irish Catholic hierarchy's policy of support for the political status quo against the interests and wishes of the vast majority of its own people must be confronted. There is an urgent need for an ongoing discussion within the Irish Catholic Church about the official Church's attitude to the consistent denial and abuse of basic rights. The discussion must inevitably deal with the right to national self-determination, the partition of Ireland and the consequences of that partition for the people of this island.

Any discussion about the future must also deal with the protection of the rights of minority groups within an Irish democracy. It is the responsibility of the Catholic hierarchy to encourage the development of a pluralistic society in which it would not interfere with minority rights or be seen to be in any way a threat to those rights.

Unionists have long objected to Irish independence on the basis that 'Home rule is Rome rule'. It is now up to the Catholic hierarchy which in the past has had an undue influence in the social and political life of the 26 counties to give the lie to that facile slogan.

Except for comments by the late Cardinal Ó Fiaich that a new constitution would be necessary for a new all-Ireland situation, discussion about the rights of minorities in a new and independent Ireland has been avoided by the Catholic hierarchy. The focus of most of the statements from Catholic Church leaders about the conflict has been condemnation of the republican movement.

The role of the Catholic hierarchy in the south has been a source of conflict and bitterness especially during and after the Mother and Child controversy. In the early 1950s the bishops prevented the then Minister for Health, Dr Noel Browne, from introducing a scheme to advise mothers about caring for children. They insisted that the state had no right to interfere in family matters.[5] The Catholic bishops have promoted an exclusively Catholic ethos in the 26 county state and have taken an extremely conservative position with regard to social legislation and the development of a pluralistic society.

In the last decade we have seen the conservative influence of the Church at work in Irish society in the 26 counties in two referenda – one amending the Constitution on abortion in 1983 and one on divorce in 1986. The Catholic hierarchy had an opportunity to show its willingness to respect the views of minorities and respect the rights of women on both these occasions but it lost the opportunity. While it could be argued that its power has been weakened since then, its still seems determined to maintain its idea of a Catholic state for a Catholic people.

The Catholic bishops have, on occasions in the past, spoken about social justice, but only in terms of those in power in London and Dublin exercising a more responsible attitude in pursuing reforms. There has been no radical analysis of the causes of conflict. There has been no questioning of the morality of the British government's claim of sovereignty in a part of Ireland. There has been no challenge to the Dublin government's acquiescence with British interference in the affairs of this country.

The bishops have never seriously questioned nor have

116

they seen the need to question the morality of the partition settlement. So long as their control over Catholic education in both states is guaranteed the Catholic hierarchy appears to have been content to support the status quo. In the past 20 years they have spoken often about the need for peace. They have never properly examined how they might make a positive contribution to the peace process nor sufficiently consulted with the victims of the system about how they could best make a positive contribution.

It is now a cliche to say that peace is not possible without justice, tolerance and respect for basic human rights. That is official Catholic teaching, as defined especially by Pope John XXIII and Pope Paul VI. The official Catholic Church, however, continues to adopt an intolerant attitude towards those who do not belong to the Catholic Church and those within the Church who do not, in conscience, accept its official teaching.

Those who maintain that Britain's involvement in Ireland must be on the agenda of any further discussions about our future represent a large section of the population in the 6 counties and a majority in Ireland and in Britain. Yet their view is not heard. It is censored and denigrated in the Irish media. The broad nationalist view that there has been unfinished business since partition is a widely-held and legitimate viewpoint and cannot be excluded by the British government or any other party or the Irish Catholic hierarchy.

If any political talks about our future are concerned only with the agenda set by the British government, they cannot lead to a lasting peace – no matter how much hype and publicity they receive and no matter how much repression and propaganda are used against the nationalist people to force them to accept a British 'solution'. This is clearly demonstrated by the lack of progress in the round of 'talks' which ended in November 1992. Talks that are not inclusive are doomed to failure.

There is an urgent need for the Catholic Church leaders to define both 'peace' and 'violence' when they use these words in their statements and sermons. They must recognise that the armed revolution in the north is taking place

117

because of the failure of the existing political system to bring about justice. The armed struggle will not be ended until an effective non-violent alternative towards achieving freedom and national self-determination is offered to the people. It is the denial of justice and the refusal of a people's birthright – the right to national self-determination – which is the primary violence and which is the cause of the republican uprising.

Peace means justice; it means respect for a people's basic rights, enshrined in laws and protected within political institutions which function justly and are recognised internationally as democratic. The British government has not made any contribution to bringing peace to this island because it does not publicly recognise its own responsibility for the conflict. It continues to manage the undemocratic statelet in the north-east – by force and military might. Peace can only come about when Britain withdraws and allows the Irish people to assert their fundamental right to independence.

The Catholic Church in Ireland must also now accept its responsibilities to those who are deprived of justice – by supporting the campaign for an end of discrimination, the end of the abuse of Catholics – and the right of the Irish people to national self-determination. They must begin to confront British violence in Ireland. Calling for the end of republican violence without at the same time calling for the ending of British violence is one-sided and politically motivated. Calling for dialogue which does not include all parties to the conflict is a recipe for further conflict.

The Catholic Church should recognise and support the non-violent work for justice that is already taking place in the face of great opposition and repression. Priests and religious should be encouraged to become involved with the people in their campaigns to end discrimination, harassment, and other injustices. This work is much more effective in building the foundations for peace than the peace and reconciliation projects which receive so much attention and public funding. These groups are acceptable to the government because they are non-threatening and because they

118

blame the victims. The campaigns on specific justice issues aim to confront the underlying violence of the state and those responsible for the maintenance of that state – the British government.

The changed attitude of the Catholic Church in some countries to the persistent violation of human rights and the denial of democracy has brought the Catholic Church in these countries into direct conflict with the political authorities. It has also split the Church. That change has come about mainly because of the pressure exerted by groups, including some priests and religious, on the Church leaders to adopt a more biblical and prophetic role and to witness to the Gospel values of justice and truth. Until that change in pastoral direction the official Church was perceived to be working in collusion with the government and the wealthy classes who were repressing and exploiting the poor.

> Without forgetting the fine examples of devotion, of sacrifice, of heroism even, we must admit that in the past – and the danger still persists – we Christians in Latin America have been, and are, seriously responsible for the situation of injustice which exists in this Continent. We have condemned the slavery of Indians and Africans; and now are we taking a sufficiently strong stand against the landowners, the rich and the powerful in our own countries? Or do we close our eyes and help to pacify their consciences, once they have camouflaged their terrible injustice by giving alms in order to build Churches (very often scandalously vast and rich, in shocking contrast with the surrounding poverty), or by contributing to our social projects?[6]

The vast majority of the Irish people are not going to give up their allegiance to the Catholic Church in the foreseeable future. They will continue to identify with and take part in the Church's liturgy. But this passive allegiance to the Church institution must be challenged so that members are forced to make a personal commitment to social justice.

Those who reject the present alliance of the Church with the state must be prepared to challenge those in the Church, including priests, who uphold that alliance. In the past republicans and other progressives have tended to avoid initiating any discussion with priests – regarding most of them as hostile to their political agenda. This has created a great gap in understanding and a breakdown in communication.

The central message of the Christian Gospel – to bring good news to the poor and oppressed – has to come into focus again in the Irish Catholic Church. The Church is meant to be a prophetic voice calling for justice and urging dialogue towards democratic solutions. Before it can be this it must make a preferential option for the cause of the poor and oppressed.

8

Meitheal Theology – A Liberation Theology for Ireland

When there is far more talk about the bishops than about the faith itself and Christ and Mary, it is time for review and reform because the institution has asserted itself over the tradition ... As the Church became more institutionalised the people handed over greater and greater responsibility to the institution. Church ruling replaced in great part the personal and conscience aspects of the faith. In the old traditional faith, there was not, perhaps, a great deal of personal decision, but there was a great deal of social decision – a mode of life and mores worked out by the people against the background of personal faith in Jesus Christ (John J Ó Riordáin, *Irish Catholic, Tradition and Transition*).

Structures and organisations are valid as a means of helping ministry in the Church, but provided they are there to serve and not be served. Structures follow sociological laws and become ends in themselves, forgetting the intentions of their founder. The spirit works by founding new base communities, from which springs new life (Jose Comblin, *The Holy Spirit and Liberation*).

Given the long colonial history of this country, it is absolutely essential to break the dependency mould in which Irish people have grown up – a legacy of British colonial rule and oppression. This dependency mould has been strengthened by the Catholic hierarchy – many of whom feel that people are not capable of making decisions, learning or planning on their own. Bishops and clergy have taken over an additional area of social control – the distribution (or withholding) of employment in Catholic areas in Belfast.

An Irish Church open to and listening to the needs and concerns of the poor could become a place where new ideas about resolving conflict and creating democracy are discussed. It could also provide facilities where those who are being harassed or tortured would find someone to document their grievances. An Irish Church concerned with the poor and oppressed could become a voice for the voiceless. It could become the defender and promoter of all human rights – including the equal rights of women.

Given the official Church's political alignment with the status quo in Ireland it is almost impossible for the official Church to be a critical or prophetic voice in Irish society. In the context of the conflict in the north the hierarchy is seen by the poor and oppressed within the Catholic community to support the British government, especially in their opposition to the MacBride principles. In the south the Catholic hierarchy is still seen by many to play a pivotal role in maintaining an unjust status quo.

Those who maintain that the official Church should be working along with the oppressed to bring an end to injustice and inequality in Ireland are in effect calling for the creation of a different model of Church. They are seeking a liberation Church of the poor, which cuts its ties with the state and the status quo. They are saying that the Church, if it is to be true to the Gospel, must show compassion and active concern for the victims of injustice. The Church through its leaders should, as it has done in some Latin American countries, make a preferential option for the poor. That would involve Catholic bishops, priests and religious making a public commitment to those who have no voice, those whose views are censored.

The Second Vatican Council defined the Church in terms of a community of equals – not a hierarchy of bishops, clergy and laity. The understanding of Church as community of equals reflects the teaching of Jesus about the Reign of God and the role of the Spirit in the life of the community. It also defines the role of ministers as people who are of service within that community basing their ministry on that of Christ. If the Catholic Church in Ireland has become clericalised, authoritarian and hierarchical then, according to the norms set down by the Vatican Council, it has lost sight of the original goal and purpose of the community formed by

Jesus as well as the ministry and teaching of Jesus himself. How is that to be recovered? Firstly, it can be achieved through education in the sense of consciousness-raising; secondly, as has happened in Latin America, through the creation of basic Christian communities among the poor; and thirdly, through increased participation of laity in Church ministry.

Traditional Catholic theology, because its focus is on doctrinal orthodoxy and because it presents Jesus as some kind of apolitical character, does not emphasise the significance of social justice and its centrality in all discussion about Christianity. Traditional theology, concerned as it is with orthodox belief, is not relevant to the situation of systematic inequality and injustice that exists in Ireland.

Neither can liberal theology – of the charismatic or the peace and reconciliation groups – offer a way forward. This kind of theology believes in a Jesus who was neutral politically and who preached a Gospel of reconciliation and peace. It ignores the Gospel of justice and liberation which seeks to confront the fundamental causes of injustice and poverty. The real division in Irish society is the economic division between rich and poor. The task confronting those who want true peace in Ireland is to remove the political and economic structures which cause inequality.

Liberation theology presents a radically different approach to poverty and injustice – because it confronts the primary cause of poverty and injustice. An Irish liberation theology will focus on the ministry and preaching of Jesus in relation to the poor and oppressed. It will not avoid the truth about his death. He died on a cross not – as Leonardo Boff reminds us – in his bed. It will demand that we today find a way forward that is as radical and as empowering as the way adopted by Jesus in his time. Liberation theology offers us that way because it approaches the issues of injustice and poverty by tackling their causes and taking the side of the powerless.

Firstly, it uses new categories for understanding the situation in terms of empowering the poor to create a new society. Secondly it is based on the notion of the Reign of

God – a notion with serious political implications in terms of confronting the status quo. Thirdly, using social sciences it offers a comprehensive understanding of the whole situation and the historical context of conflict and injustice as seen from the viewpoint of the poor.

> Medieval and Reformation theology emphasised the distinction of natural and supernatural worlds, separate worlds of secular and divine activity, worlds that did not always have much to do with one another ... This distinction was denied by the Second Vatican Council and the consequent affirmation of the unity of history has become the major rationale for the involvement of the Latin American Church in the social and political world. The shift in perspective from an other-worldly to a this-worldly perspective is extreme.[1]

Fourthly, it refers to social sin and social morality – the application of Gospel values to society and to the social and political structures. It does not deal only with individual and personal morality. It proposes new ways of living one's commitment to the Gospel and working for social change. It is the alternative way that the Church offers to those who have despaired that violent means of bringing about change was their only recourse.

All members of the Church are called to make a preferential option for the poor. This is not just a pastoral option – but a political option as well. It will mean confronting those in power – some of whom also belong to the same Church or to other Christian Churches, and who are responsible for poverty and torture. It will mean preaching about injustice and the need to take effective action to eradicate specific instances of these injustices.

Those within the Irish Catholic Church who decide to make a preferential option for the poor and oppressed are challenging the alliance of the official Catholic Church with the status quo. They challenge both the traditional conservative theology and the liberal theology of those who refuse to challenge the unjust status quo but who often use the language of liberation theology.

A theology of liberation sees the need for social analysis

124

if we are to understand anything of the reasons for the conflict in our society or the growing gap between rich and poor. The traditional or dominant theology of the Catholic Church in Ireland has ignored the need for social analysis. The liberal theology does not accept its necessity either.

Irish Catholics have had a strong devotion to Mary. Liberation theology stresses the role of Mary in God's work of liberation. We read in the Gospels that Mary, the mother of Jesus, identified the causes of inequality in her society. She did her own social analysis – and she accepted that done by the prophets who identified injustice and oppression by the rich and mighty as the cause of poverty. She spoke of the gap between the rich and the poor. In this regard Mary was a revolutionary; she thought about the situation and she identified the causes of injustice:

> You have shown the power of your arm,
> You have routed the proud of heart.
> You have pulled down princes from their thrones
> and exalted the lowly.
> The hungry you have filled with good things,
> the rich sent empty away (Lk. 1:39).

Jesus, learning from Mary, also analysed the causes of poverty and oppression in the society in which he lived as did the prophets before him – Isaiah and Amos, etc.

A similar kind of analysis must be carried out with regard to the social and political institutions in Ireland today. The word of God as interpreted by the oppressed is the beginning of a social analysis. That is why Bible study and small group discussion are important. The Bible must be read through the eyes of the poor and oppressed if it is to be correctly understood. Such an analysis identifies the causes of people's poverty and oppression – the greed of the rich. It is concerned with everyday issues like exploitation of workers, the humiliation of those on the dole – harassment, torture of those in police custody, discrimination, etc.

In the past the Church hierarchy has adopted a narrow interpretation of human rights. The right to life in the context of a struggle for liberation is understood as the right to all the basic necessities for a full and rich life. That requires just and efficient political and economic structures. People have the right, not only to life, but to the means to live useful and productive lives.

A major problem from the point of view of the poor in Ireland is that bishops and priests have become identified with the middle-class and the affluent in society. Because of their education and social background the clergy tend to see the world through middle-class eyes rather than from the perspective of the poor. Priests are educated and groomed to feel apart from, above, the oppressed community. They can tell them what to do because they know better. They preach and talk about religion through middle-class eyes and using middle-class language. In doing so they confirm the views of the middle-class in Ireland about being respectable and they further isolate and alienate the poor.

Priests who have the task of preaching the good news are being called to make friends with poor people; to re-read the Scriptures with them, listening to their views and interpretation. They are challenged to learn the language of the poor and to live and work with the poor.

The role of the priest will be redefined primarily in terms of the prophetic ministry of the priesthood:

> I'm a priest, an evangeliser. And if my evangelising role has political consequences that serve the people's liberation so be it.[2]

Gustavo Gutierrez speaks about his pastoral ministry:

> I think that to be committed to the poor is to have friends among the poor. It is not enough to say you are committed to the poor as a culture. You must be committed to real persons and to be living among them ... If we do not have friendships with actual persons I don't think we are really committed to them. We must try to live with them.[3]

The Irish Catholic Church has had a long missionary tradition – since the early Celtic Church. Irish missionaries went off to preach the Gospels and make converts and soon discovered that charity is not the answer to situations of deep-seated injustice.

Learning from the experience in Latin America, South Africa and Asia as well as from our own experience, Catholics in Ireland can work out a strategy to create a Church which will make a clear preferential option for the poor and the powerless in this country. That strategy will involve establishing a network of base Christian communities among the poor throughout this country – communities which are committed above all to social justice and equality.

A Church committed to seeking justice, educating for liberation and consisting of basic communities offers those who are alienated from the Catholic Church some hope. It offers people an active role within a Christian scriptural context in opposing injustice and oppression in Irish society. The Church of the Poor is based on the new understanding of Church presented in the Second Vatican Council as a community of equals and a community in solidarity with the poor and oppressed. It is founded on the Gospel ministry of Jesus as someone totally committed to the poor and oppressed, and to their liberation – so much so that he was prepared to give his life in this cause.

The Irish Catholic bishops have made statements about poverty and unemployment – but they have not yet seriously confronted the root causes of poverty and those responsible. They will have to confront the governments in London and Dublin about their social, economic and political policies which have such dire consequences for the poor in both states in Ireland. When they do they will show a real commitment to ending poverty, injustice and chronic unemployment in Ireland.

The Church, which is called to be the prophetic voice announcing the good news about the community of truth and justice, is obliged to confront and challenge any government which does not abide by international agreements on the protection of human rights and sovereignty. Amnesty International and Helsinki Watch have reported on the persistent violation of the rights of people in the north of Ireland by the British government. The Catholic bishops have remained silent.

The official Church could only be an effective critic of governments if the Church itself is seen as a community which respects the human dignity and freedom of its own members. This is best achieved when people are given a say and encouraged to participate – when the people have power in the Church. The poor are always the main agents of change in the Church and in society, through their skills and imagination. So far they have been allowed little say in the Irish Church.

The work for justice in Ireland could be carried out effectively within small groups of marginalised people whose members reflect on the Bible and its meaning for their situation. It is not done in the privacy and security of a study removed from the reality of life for the working class. A new Irish theology will be created by those in Ireland who are involved in the various campaigns for justice and human rights. It could be based on the Irish tradition of neighbour helping neighbour – the *meitheal*. Irish liberation theology could be a *meitheal* theology. The Catholic clergy must make available their buildings and parish resources to all those groups throughout Ireland which are working for justice and change – instead of playing it safe lest they fall out of favour with those who support the status quo.

In the last twenty years the gap between rich and poor in Ireland has widened considerably – but the Catholic clergy have remained on the side of the better off rather than taking up the cause of the poor. The Catholic middle-class has become well established in Ireland and has a great deal of power, wealth and political influence. They would wish to use the Church for their purposes and adapt the Church to their needs.

The option facing the Irish Catholic Church hierarchy is to accept the challenge posed by the poor in our country or to continue to be part of the establishment. They can, of course, make the occasional ritualistic statements about social justice, unemployment and opting for the poor but they will make no effective contribution to ending poverty and injustice unless they act in solidarity with the poor and oppressed at all times and refuse to allow themselves to be co-opted by any government.

The early Irish Church was, in its make-up and pastoral approach, more akin to the basic communities that exist in the Church in Latin America today. It was open, vibrant, responsive to the needs of the poor and oppressed. Its spirituality was creation-centred. It was a community-oriented organisation. It could have been out of this strong community awareness that the practice of meitheal became so widespread.

The Church of the Penal Times in Ireland was a persecuted Church – where priests and bishops lived in solidarity and suffered with the poor and oppressed. The authoritarian model of Church which supports and defends the status quo in Ireland today is not acceptable especially when a large section of the population is living in poverty and when those who seek to bring about social change are being marginalised and harrassed by government forces. Recent statements by the bishops in the west of Ireland indicate a willingness by some to tackle the serious economic situation facing the people in the western part of this island. It remains to be seen what impact their initiatives will have.

There has to be a radical break with the past political and social alignments if there is to be a process of renewal in the Irish Church. The official Church must give up its attachment to the status quo and its alliance with the rich and powerful in Irish society. It must become a Church concerned about and involved in the daily realities of life of the poor. Only a Church of the Poor, actively engaged in the lives of the poor and oppressed, demanding justice and equality by confronting those in power, will be a prophetic witness to the Gospel of Christ.

Conclusion

The Church stands ever in need of evangelisation (Pope Paul VI).

But who is to evangelise the Church – its governing body, the hierarchy? (L. Boff).

It is important to realise that the true subjects of the liberation of the poor must be the poor themselves. All our works must try to contribute to helping the poor take their history and their destiny into their own hands. The question is not only to establish a more just society but to ensure that this is the task of the poor themselves. Therefore the goal is to work with the poor and help them to be more conscious of the reasons for their poverty and to look for some solution. But the poor are the subjects of their history. That is a central and important point in liberation (Gustavo Gutierrez, *The Other Side*).

It is one of the arguments of this book that the growing poverty and inequality in Ireland cannot be properly understood – or dealt with – outside the context of partition. This situation makes special demands of the Irish Catholic Church which has for so long accepted the status quo. One can examine inequities in the 26 counties as well as in the 6 counties but one cannot ignore the fact that the most critical factor giving rise to these inequities in both unnatural subdivisions is the partition of this island. Some people prefer to talk about the need for good community relations. They avoid the issue which makes good community relations impossible – the British government's involvement in Irish affairs and the historic reliance on fractionalising the Irish people as a political strategy.

While the growing gap between rich and poor in Ireland has been recognised by the official Catholic Church it is not surprising that it has not come up with a more radical analysis of the reasons for the inequality nor a coherent strategy for change. A more critical understanding of the role of the Church in society is essential – indeed, crucial – if there is to

130

be any change in how the Irish hierarchy perceives its role in relation to injustice and inequality within Ireland. There is also need for radical change within the Church itself.

Within the Catholic Church in Ireland there is little room for dissent or even discussion. It is a class-based Church where the well-off middle-class have the most say. The poor, the so-called 'ordinary people', are never consulted or listened to except in a paternalistic way.

The bishops and priests are mostly cut off from the poorer section of the community – living a relatively privileged middle-class lifestyle. The conservative theological formation and training of the clergy and the traditional undemocratic parish structures do not encourage any real pastoral interaction with the poor. One of the consequences is that official spokesmen for the Church are often insensitive to the needs and feelings of the poor and oppressed and are sometimes heard blaming the people for their own plight.

The relationship of the Catholic Church in Ireland to the state is not unique. In some other countries the Church pursued a similar role of supporting the status quo – even when it was blatantly unjust. In many former colonies and dictatorships the official Church had become closely aligned with the status quo – legitimising the injustice and oppression of dictators and colonial governments. However, in some of these countries a new model of Church has emerged – a Church which is challenging the traditional support given by bishops and clergy to unjust governments.

As a result of the growth of liberation theology and the basic Christian communities there now exists in some countries in Latin America, Africa and Asia, a Church within a Church – a Church of the poor and oppressed within the official Church of the powerful. This has resulted in a great deal of tension and conflict because the Church of the Poor is feared by those in Rome who still believe that it is in the Church's best interests to identify with the state. They fear that it may challenge the political and social elites in the different countries.

In Ireland the official Irish Catholic Church appears to

be most unwilling to give up its close alliance with the status quo or to allow the poor any real say. This is in contradiction to the Church's own official teaching. The Second Vatican Council stressed the need for the Church to adopt a less hierarchical and authoritarian style of government.

The Christian faith in Ireland is still presented most often as an individual matter about 'saving your soul' and about getting on with your neighbour, without making any radical political demands. The faithful are expected to be 'good and loyal citizens' and to continue giving alms to the 'poor' and allegiance to the state – no matter what that state does.

It is typical of institutional religion that attention is focused on the person in authority. He is seen or proclaimed as the bearer of truth, the guide, the one to be obeyed. There is very considerable emphasis on structure, hierarchy and other expressions of the institution in the presentation of religion.

It is my contention in this book that the Irish Church has lost sight of its original mission – 'to bring good news to the poor, to set the downtrodden free'. It is preoccupied with its buildings, property, schools and above all its image as protector of establishment values and the status quo. Instead of fighting for justice for the poor and oppressed and tackling the political causes of poverty the Catholic hierarchy is, by its silence about the root causes, legitimising and bolstering the status quo. Efforts to appear relevant through the publication of statements about unemployment are not sufficient if the Church is not seen to be involved in the struggles and campaigns of the poor and oppressed.

The documents of the Second Vatican Council, especially the document *Gaudium et Spes* or 'The Church in the World', have outlined the need for reform and change within the Catholic Church and its mission to be a prophetic voice in society. A prophetic Church would address the causes of injustice and oppression in society and seek alternative ways of dealing with conflict. It is clear that in order to do this effectively the Church would have to adopt a stance where it could be free to criticise governments and their agents in the civil service. While Catholic bishops are involved in state-sponsored schemes and receiving government funding, it is difficult to see how they can become prophetic voices.

If the Irish Catholic Church is to address its responsibilities in an effective and meaningful way then the hierarchy must give up its alliance with the state and build an alliance with those who are oppressed. Because of the support given the status quo in Ireland by the hierarchy a large section of the Catholic community – especially in the most neglected parts of the large cities and towns – has become alienated from the official Church. Some have become cynical about the Church. Some are angry when Churchmen tell people how to vote or how not to vote. Many are disillusioned with the double standards.

It is true to say that it is not only the poor who feel alienated from the Church. There is another level of alienation where a section of the middle class have become increasingly disaffected by the stance of the Church on many issues like divorce, contraception, women priests and compulsory celibacy. However, in this book, I am concerned with the alienation of the poor.

It is clear that a radical change in the pastoral approach of the Irish Catholic Church is unlikely to come from the top. Experience shows that, as far as large institutions are concerned, change seldom happens that way. The official Irish Church has not encouraged any critical theological discussion. There is little by way of experimentation or innovation within parishes to show the Church's concern for the poor and its opposition to social injustice. It is now the task of the poor in Ireland to evangelise the Church, to convert the Church to its true role and proper mission. As Leonardo Boff states:

Indeed, it is the poor who today must evangelise the theologians, priests, religious and bishops. They evangelise by what is proper to them and what was grasped so well by the whole Old Testament: by their outcry against injustice, their demand for liberation, by the call for solidarity provoked by their misery, by their will to participation, that they may be the agents of their history and of the Church community.[1]

If there is to be an open and progressive Church in Ireland concerned with bringing about social justice it will grow up among those people throughout the country who are prepared to take up the issue of social justice. Concerned people, in every diocese, will have to question the clergy and religious about their stance – and challenge the traditional political alliance of the official Irish Catholic Church with the status quo.

The Irish Catholic Church must be changed from being a Church of 'the respectable' and the powerful to become a Church of the poor and powerless, a Church concerned with the issue of institutional violence as well as the victims of state violence. If it is to have any credibility as a Christian Church it must identify with the poor; their concerns must become the major concerns of the whole Church. It must be free to challenge those in power about their unjust policies. It must give up its property and possessions to the poor and it must re-examine its involvement in controlling education and giving moral sanction to the prevailing 'property' values.

When we look at the compliant role adopted by the official Catholic Church in Ireland during the past two centuries we see the urgent need for an Irish liberation theology that will force the official Church to make a radical break with past alliances – a theology that will free the Church from its imprisonment to the status quo.

The creation of an Irish liberation theology is the best hope for the growth of a renewed and vibrant Church in this country. It is the only way that the Church will be able to analyse and address the ongoing tragic conflict in the northeast of our country, as well as the growing gap between rich and poor throughout the whole island. It is the only way that the disillusionment and anger of many with the current pastoral approach of the official Church can be turned to hope and positive action.

There needs to be a continuing discussion within the Church – involving all concerned members about issues of oppression and injustice. As a result of open discussion and dialogue the people would be helping to create a new, open, compassionate Church in Ireland – a Church that is clearly seen to stand in solidarity with the poor – not with the state or any government. If members of the Church hierarchy were to welcome and encourage open discussion between clergy and the marginalised, it might halt the increasing alienation and prevent any further unnecessary bitterness.

The Gospel, when read and interpreted by the poor and oppressed, has important political implications which in Ireland, as elsewhere, mean facing up to the root causes of poverty and violence in our society and confronting those in power who are responsible.

Christian morality is distinguished by the vision it has of a society where the poor and oppressed are treated with dignity and respect and where basic human rights are vigorously promoted and upheld. To live morally, according to the Christian way, is to pursue those values which promote human dignity. That must inevitably bring committed Christians into conflict with governments which flout basic human rights.

If Jesus were to walk among the people of Ireland today he would surely be using the basic arguments of liberation theology (not just the language which anyone can use) to confront those who use religion (with his name) for their own ends in order to uphold the corrupt status quo. He would, I believe, try to renew the people's faith in the God who defends and supports the poor. He would remind them of the power that is within them to bring about radical change.

The God of the Bible, 'Yahweh', was the God of the poor who anointed Moses to lead the people out of slavery in Egypt to the Promised Land. Yahweh, the God of the Old Testament, is the God of Jesus who identified with the poor and the marginalised in Galilee. In Ireland today, those with a vested interest in maintaining the status quo have replaced the God of Life and Justice with a 'god of obedience' – an idol. Idolatry is not a thing of the past. That is why if Jesus

135

came to live in Ireland today he would again be persecuted – and his followers would suffer persecution and harassment at the hands of so-called religious people in church and state – conservatives and liberals.

Christian morality, which derives from the belief in the power of God's presence in creation confronts people with the basic demands of being human, of living together as equals and working to create justice. Christian faith urges people and empowers people to work together to make this vision a reality by tackling the causes of injustice.

In Ireland much of the Catholic religion is geared to ritual and private devotion. Seeking justice/democracy and opposing injustice and political corruption is not seen by many Catholics as the most essential and important demand of their religious faith. And yet it is at the heart of both the Old Testament faith and the teaching of Jesus. It is at the heart of Christian morality and Christian ethics.

The prophets of the Old Testament denounced ritual, prayer and religious practice which was not concerned with correcting oppression. The Church (which includes all of the members) is here to promote God's justice. This idea, with its origins in the Old Testament, is at the heart of the message of Jesus. It was a commitment to the struggle for justice which he inaugurated by his life and ministry. We cannot properly understand Jesus or the Church or Christian morality without understanding the social and political implications of the Reign of God as preached by Jesus.

In Irish Catholic preaching and teaching, there is a strong emphasis on personal piety and on personal morality. There is nothing wrong with this if it also includes a commitment to justice and leads to the building of a Christian community which is committed to the struggle of the poor, following the example of Jesus. He disturbed rather than smoothed the rich and powerful in his day. He distinguished between false peace based on security and true peace which is based on justice.

A sense of outrage and anger about the exploitation and manipulation of the poor in Ireland is missing in the official Irish Catholic version of Christianity. It is missing in the

Pastorals and the preaching. It is missing in the statements and the interviews and therefore, the statements do not translate into radical action. The Biblical God of the Exodus is angry at how the people were treated by those in power. Irish people have suffered centuries of slavery, oppression and marginalisation. But they do not know about this God. They are not told about this God – and they do not hear because the Catholic Church in Ireland is aligned with the political and economic status quo.

We need to develop this sense of anger and outrage to show real solidarity with the poor and oppressed.

We need to be honest about the political corruption and structural injustice that exists in Ireland today. There is much dishonesty among Catholics – especially those who are always talking about 'peace and reconciliation'. The Catholic Church in Ireland needs to face up to its responsibilities and its mistakes, above all its policy of colluding with the oppressors. It has a special responsibility to speak the truth and to identify the causes of inequality and poverty.

There is now an opportunity for those who are committed to renewing the Irish Church to create a new theology that is concerned with bringing about justice and equality as the only basis for true peace and reconciliation on this island.

Notes

Chapter 1

1. Gustavo Gutierrez, *The God of Life*, SCM, 1991, pp. XV ff.
2. Jorge Pixley and Clodovis Boff, *The Bible, the Church and the Poor*, p. 17-18.
3. Albert Nolan, 'Taking Sides', CIIR pamphlet, p. 8.

Chapter 2

1. *Maryknoll Magazine*, January 1986, p. 84.
2. Paul N Siegel, *The Meek and the Militant*, p. 84.
3. Louie Hechanova, 'The Gospel and the Struggle', CIIR pamphlet 1986.
4. *The Gospel in Soltentiname*, Five volumes, Orbis, Maryknoll 1984.
5. C Avila, *Ownership, Early Christian Teaching*, p. 94.
6. *Ibid.*, p. 132.
7. *Ibid.*, p. 64.
8. *Ibid.*, p. 81.
9. *Ibid.*, pp. 136-137.
10. *Ibid.*, pp. 137-138.
11. Gustavo Gutierrez in *Readings in Christian Theology* p. 259-260.
12. Bartolme de Las Casas was once an unjust landowner but was converted and defended the native Indians in Nicaragua. He wrote that Indians were treated like 'sticks, stones, cats or dogs ... even beasts enjoy more freedom'. *c.f.* Veritas pamphlet.
13. P Berryman, *Liberation Theology*, p. 94.
14. J O'Brien and T A Shannon (Ed.), *Renewing the Earth*, p. 40.
15. Pixley and Boff, p. 183.
16. *Ibid.*, p. 137.
17. Pope John Paul II's Lenten Message 1991 (Irish Ordo 1991).
18. Boff, L and Elizondo, V (Ed.), 'Theology from the Viewpoint of the Poor' in *Concilium*, p. xiii.
19. Penny Lernoux, *People of God*, p. 212.
20. Dermot Lane, *Foundations for a Social Theology*, p. 142.
21. Jack Nelson-Pallmeyer, *The Politics of Compassion*, p. 14.
22. *Latin America Press*, Lima, Peru, October 1984.
23. *Ibid.*, p. 7.

Chapter 3

1. John Gerasi (Ed.), *Camillo Torres, Revolutionary Priest*, p. 325.
2. *Ibid.*, p. 331.
3. P Berryman, *Liberation Theology*, Taurus 1987, p. 19.
4. *Maryknoll Magazine*, April 1987.
5. Ellis and Maduro (Ed.), *Expanding the View, the Writings of Gustavo Gutierrez*, p. 196.
6. J Nelson-Pallmeyer, *War Against the Poor*, p. 15.
7. Jose Comblin, *Being Human*, p. 38.
8. Paulo Freire, *Pedagogy of the Oppressed and other Writings*.
9. P Berryman, *Liberation Theology*, p. 23.
10. MacEoin G and Riley N, *Puebla: A Church Being Born*, p. 327.

11. *Ibid.*, p. 68.
12. *Catholic New York* – a weekly paper, 3 Jan, 1985.
13. *The Other Side* – a monthly magazine, November 1987.
14. M R Candeleira, *Popular Religion and Liberation*, p. 125.
15. Carlos Mester's article in *The Bible and Liberation*, (Ed.) Norman K Gottwald, p. 119 ff.
16. Enrique Batangan, CIIR pamphlet, 'Faith and Social Change', 1985.
17. *Catholic New York*, 3 Jan, 1985.
18. P Berryman, *Liberation Theology*, p. 70-71.
19. *Ibid.*, p. 71.
20. Andrew Bradstock, *Saints and Sandinistas*, p. 42
21. *Ibid.*, p. 60.
22. *Ibid.*, p. 64.
23. *Ibid.*, p. 64.
24. T Cabesterero, *Ministers of God, Ministers of the People*, pp. 129-130.
25. D Barbé, *Grace and Power*, p. 20.
26. Leonardo Boff, *When Theology Listens to the Poor*, p. 12.

Chapter 4
1. Peter Beresford Ellis, *A History of the Irish Working Class*, p. 19.
2. Hughes and Hamlin, *The Modern Traveller to the Early Irish Church*, p. 17.
3. Shirley Toulson, *The Celtic Alternative*, p. 112.
4. Seán MacReamoinn (Ed.), *The Pleasures of Gaelic Poetry*, p. 27.
5. D Ó Laoghaire, 'Irish Spirituality', pamphlet, Gill and Macmillan.
6. Toulson, p. 3.
7. Hughes and Hamlin, p. 13.
8. Liz Curtis, *Nothing but the same old Story*, p. 8.
9. Ellis, p. 27.
10. Canice Mooney, *The Church in Gaelic Ireland*, p. 3.
11. Gerald of Wales, *The History and Topography of Ireland*, (Ed.) O'Meara.
12. Curtis, p. 11.
13. Curtis, p. 15.
14. Curtis, p. 17.
15. Maureen Wall, *The Penal Laws*.
16. James Coombes, *A Bishop of the Penal Times*, p. 109-110.
17. *Seanchas Ard Mhaca*, Vol 5, No 2 1970, article by Rev Brendan McEvoy.
18. Hansard, 1854 (Richard Lawlor Shiels).
19. Peter O'Leary, *My Story*, (translated by C Ó Céirín), p. 56.
20. *Ibid.*, Appendix IX.
21. Michael J F McCarthy, *Priests and People in Ireland* (1903) pp. 40-41.
22. Rosemary Radford Reuther, *Contemporary Roman Catholicism*, p. vii.
23. Paul Blanshard, *The Irish and Catholic Power*, p. 87.
24. Margaret Gralton, *My Cousin Jimmy*, p. 17.
25. *Ibid.*, p. 18.
26. *Ibid.*, p. 19.
27. William Nolan and Kevin Whelan (Ed.), *Kilkenny History and Society* – article by Anna Brennan and William Nolan, p. 579.
28. *Ibid.*, pp. 580-581.
29. John J Ó Riordáin, *Irish Catholics, Tradition and Transition*, pp. 1-2.

Chapter 5

1. James J Whitehead, *Being a Priest Today*, ed Donald J Goergen, p. 27.
2. *Ibid.*, p. 26.
3. *Ibid.*, p. 26.
4. *Ibid.*, p. 27.
5. *Ibid.*, p. 27.
6. The Irish Bishops Pastoral, *The Work of Justice*, p. 48.
7. *Ibid.*, p. 55.
8. The Irish Epsicopal Conference, *Work is the Key*.
9. James Cone, *God of the Oppressed*, p. 128.

Chapter 6

1. Carey Oppenheim, *Poverty, the Facts*, p. 5.
2. *Ibid.*, p. 7.
3. *Ibid.* p. 7.
4. *Ibid.*, p. 8.
5. Northern Ireland Economic and Research Centre Report (1991).
6. *Ibid.*
7. CMRS 1990 Budget Response, p. 3.
8. Child Action Group Report 1990.
9. 1989 CMRS pre-Budget submission.
10. *Unemployment, Jobs and the 1990s.*

Chapter 7

1. Flann Campbell, *The Dissenting Voice*, p. 7.
2. Robert Heatley, *Breaking the Deadlock*, p. 7.
3. The Brian Nelson Case, *Irish News*, January 1992.
4. *Irish News*, 27 September 1991.
5. Noel Browne, *Against the Tide*, p. 141.
6. Helder Camara, *The Church and Colonialism*, p. 103 ff.

Chapter 8

1. T. Cabestrero, *Ministers of God, Ministers of the People*, p. ix.
2. Gustavo Gutierrez, Interview, *The Other Side*, November 1987, p. 13.
3. *Ibid.*, p. 13.

Conclusion

1. Leonardo Boff, *Good News to the Poor*.

Bibliography

Araya, Victorio, *God of the Poor*, Orbis, Maryknoll, New York, 1987.

Aristide, Jean-Bertrand, *In the Parish of the Poor*, Orbis, Maryknoll, New York 1990.

Avila, Charles, *Ownership – Early Christian Teaching*, Orbis, Maryknoll, New York and Sheed and Ward, London 1983.

Bacik, James J, *Contemporary Theologians*, Mercier Press, Cork and Dublin 1989.

Banana, Canaan, *The Gospel according to the Ghetto*, Mambi Press Zimbabwe 1981.

Barbe, Dominique, *Grace and Power*, Orbis, Maryknoll, New York 1987.

Barbe, Dominique, *A Theology of Conflict and* other *Writings on Non-violence*, Orbis, Maryknoll, New York 1989.

de Baróid, Ciaran, *Ballymurphy and the Irish War*, Aisling Publications, Dublin 1989.

Batstone, David, *From Conquest to Struggle*, SUNY Press, Albany New York 1991.

Berryman, Philip, *Liberation Theology*, I. B. Taurus, London 1987.

Berryman, Philip, *The Religious Roots of Rebellion*, SCM Ltd, London 1984.

Blanshard, Paul, *The Irish and Catholic Power*, Verschoyle, London 1984.

Boff, Leonardo, *Good News to the Poor*, Burns and Oates, Tunbridge Wells and Orbis Books, Maryknoll, New York 1982.

Boff, Leonardo, *The Lord's Prayer*, Orbis, Maryknoll, New York 1983.

Boff, Leonardo, *When Theology Listens to the Poor*, Harper and Row, San Francisco 1988.

Boff, Leonardo, *Church, Charism and Power*, SCM London 1985.

Boff, Leonardo, *Jesus Christ Liberator*, Orbis Books, Maryknoll, New York 1981.

Boff, Leonardo, Clodovis, *Salvation and Liberation*, Orbis, Maryknoll, New York 1984.

Boff, Leonardo and Virgil Elizondo, *Concilium – Option for the Poor*, Clark, Edinburgh 1986.

Bradstock, Andrew, *Saints and Sandinistas*, Epworth Press, London 1987.

de Breffny, Brian (Ed)., *The Irish World*, Thames and Hudson, London 1977.

Bredin, Eamonn, *Disturbing the Peace*, Columba Press, Dublin 1985.

Brockman, James R, *The Word Remains: A Life of Oscar Romero*, Orbis, Maryknoll, New York 1982.

Brockman, James R, *The Church is all of you: Thoughts of Archbishop Romero*, Winston Press, Minneapolis 1984.

Browne, Noel, *Against the Tide*, Gill and Macmillan, Dublin 1986.

Burke, Maurice, *Britain in Ireland: The Facts*, Oisin Publications, Bogota, New Jersey 1990.

Cabestrero, Teofilo, *Ministers of God, Ministers of the People*, Orbis, Maryknoll, New York 1983.

Camara, Dom Helder, *The Church and Colonialism*, Dimension Books, Denville, New Jersey 1969.

141

Campbell, Flann, *The Dissenting Voice*, Blackstaff, Belfast 1991.

Candeleria, Michael R, *Popular Religion and Liberation – the Dilemma of Liberation Theology*, SUNY Press, Albany New York 1990.

Carroll, Denis, *What is Liberation Theology?* Mercier Press, Dublin/Fowler Wright Books, Leominster 1987.

Cleary, Edward L, *Crisis and Change – The Church in Latin America Today*, Maryknoll, New York 1985.

Comblin, Jose, *Being Human – a Christian Anthropology*, Burns and Oates, London 1990.

Comblin, Jose, *The Holy Spirit and Liberation*, Burns and Oates, Tunbridge Wells, 1989.

Cone, James, *God of the Oppressed*, Harper and Row, San Francisco 1975.

Connolly, James, *Labour in Irish History*, New Books Publications, Dublin 1983.

Coombes, James, *A Bishop of Penal Times*, Tower Books of Cork, Cork 1981.

Crotty, Raymond, *Ireland in Crisis*, Brandon Books Ltd, Dingle 1986.

Cullen, L M, *An Economic History of Ireland since 1660*, B T Batsford, London 1976.

Curtis, Liz, *Ireland and the Propaganda War*, Pluto Press, London and Sydney 1984.

Curtis, Liz, *Nothing but the Same Old Story*, Information on Ireland, London 1984.

Doyle, Dennis M, *The Church Emerging from Vatican II*, 23rd Publications, Mystic, 1992.

Douthwaite, Richard, *The Growth Illusion*, The Lilliput Press, Dublin 1992.

Ellis, Peter Beresford, *A History of the Irish Working Class*, Pluto Press, London and Sydney 1985.

Ellis, Marc H and Otto Manduro, *Expanding the View – Gustavo Gutierrez and the Future of Liberation Theology*, Orbis, Maryknoll, New York 1988.

Evason, Eileen, *Ends that won't meet – a Study of Poverty in Belfast*, Child Poverty Action Group, London 1980.

Farrell, Michael, *The Orange State*, Pluto Press, London and Sydney 1980.

Ferm, Deane William, *Third World Liberation Theologies*, Orbis Maryknoll, New York 1986.

Gerasi, John (ed) *Revolutionary Priest – the Complete Writings of Camilo Torres*, Vintage Books, New York 1971.

Gerald of Wales, *The History and Topography of Ireland*, Penguin Classics, London 1982.

Goergen, Donald J (Ed), *Being a Priest Today*, Liturgical Press, Collegeville, Minnesota 1992.

Gottwald, Norman K, *The Bible and Liberation*, Orbis, Maryknoll, New York 1984.

Gralton, Margaret, *My Cousin Jimmy*, Drumlin Publications, Sligo. 1985.

Greaves, C Desmond, *The Life and Times of James Connolly*, Lawrence and Wishart, London 1961.

Greene, David and Frank O'Connor (eds), *Golden Treasury of Irish Poetry AD 600-1200*, Brandon, Dingle 1990.

Gutierrez, Gustavo, *A Theology of Liberation*, Orbis, New York 1973.

142

Gutierrez, Gustavo, *The Power of the Poor in History*, SCM, London 1983.

Gutierrez, Gustavo, *The God of Life*, SCM London 1991.

Guttierez, Gustavo, *We Drink from our own Wells*, Orbis, New York 1984.

Haughey, John (Ed), *The Faith that does Justice*, Paulist Press, New York 1977.

Heatley, Robert, *Breaking the Deadlock, Campaign for Democracy* (Belfast) and Fulcrum Press, Dublin 1991.

Hoornart, Eduardo, *The Memory of the Christian People*, Orbis, New York 1988.

Hughes, Kathleen, *The Church in Early Irish Society*, Methuen, London 1966.

Kirby, Peadar, *Has Ireland a Future?*, Mercier Press, Cork and Dublin 1988.

Lernoux, Penny, *Cry of the People*, Penguin, New York 1982.

Lernoux, Penny, *People of God*, Viking Penguin, New York 1982.

Maher, Michael (Ed), *Irish Spirituality*, Veritas, Dublin 1981.

McBrien, Richard P, *Ministry*, Harper and Row, San Francisco 1988.

McCarthy, Michael, *Priests and People in Ireland*, Hodges Figgis and Co Ltd, London 1903.

McCormack V, and O'Hara J, *Enduring Inequality*, Liberty, London 1990.

MacEoin, G and Riley N, *Puebla: A Church Bring Born*, Paulist Press, New York, 1980

Memmi, Albert, *The Coloniser and the Colonised*, Earthscan, London 1990.

Mesters, Carlos, *The Road to Freedom*, Veritas, Dublin 1974.

Moltmann, Jurgen, *The Trinity and the Kingdom* of *God*, SCM Press Ltd, London 1983.

Moody, TW and Martin FX (Eds), *The Course of Irish History*, Mercier Press, Cork and Dublin 1987.

Nelson-Pallmeyer, Jack, *The Politics of Compassion*, Orbis, Maryknoll, New York 1984.

Nolan, Albert, *Jesus before Christianity – the Gospels of Liberation*, Darton, Longman and Todd Ltd, London 1977.

O'Brien, John, *Theology and the Options for the Poor*, Collegeville, 1992.

O'Brien, David J and Thomas A Shannon, *Renewing the Earth, Catholic Documents on Peace, Justice and Liberation*, Image Books, Garden City, New York 1977.

Ó Fiaich, Tomás, *Columbanus in his Own Words*, Veritas, Dublin 1974.

O'Halloran, James, *Signs of Hope*, Orbis, Maryknoll, New York 1991.

O'Halloran, James, *Living Cells*, Orbis, Maryknoll, New York 1984.

Ó hEithir, Breandan, *The Begrudger's Guide to Irish Politics*, Poolbeg 1986.

O'Leary, Canon Peter, *My Story*, Oxford University Press, Oxford and New York 1987.

Ó Riordáin, John J, *Irish Catholics, Tradition and Transition*, Veritas, Dublin 1980.

Oppenheim, Carey, *Poverty, the Facts*, Child Poverty Action Group, London 1990.

Peillon, Michel, *Contemporary Irish Society – an Introduction*, Gill and Macmillan, Dublin 1982.

Pixley, J and Boff, C *The Bible, the Church and the Poor*, trans. by Paul Burns, Burns and Oates, Tunbridge Wells 1989.

Radford-Reuther, Rosemary, *Contemporary Catholicism – Crises and*

Challenges, Sheed and Ward, Kansas, 1987.

Rohr, Richard, *Simplicity – the Art of Living*, Crossroad, New York, 1992.

Rowthorn, Bob and Naomi Wayne, *Northern Ireland – the Political Economy of Conflict*, Polity Press, Cambridge 1988.

Seigel, Paul N, *The Meek and the Militant – Religion and Power Across the World*, Zed Books, London and New York 1986.

Stegemann, Wolfgang, *The Gospel and the Poor*, Fortress press, PA 1984.

Torres, Sergio and John Eagleson (Eds), *The Challenge of Basic Christian Communities*, Orbis Maryknoll, New York 1981.

Toulson, Shirley, *The Celtic Alternative – the Christianity We Lost*, Rider, London 1987.

de Waal, Esther, *A World made Whole*, Fount, London 1991.

Wall, Maureen, *The Penal Laws 1691-1760*, Dublin Historical Association, Dublin 1976.

Walsh, John J, *Integral Justice*, Orbis, Maryknoll, New York 1990.

Walshe, Peter, *The Evolution of Liberation Theology in South Africa*, The Journal of Law and Religion, Vol IV, no 2, 1987.

Whitehead, James D and Whitehead, Evelyn, *The Emerging Laity*, Image, New York 1988.

Whitehead, James D and Whitehead, Evelyn, *Community of Faith*, Twenty-Third Publications, Mystic, Connecticut 1992.

Whyte, J H, *Church and State in Modern Ireland 1923-1979*, Gill and Macmillan, Dublin 1984.

Wilson, Robert and Donovan Wylie, *The Dispossessed*, Pan Books Ltd, London 1992.

Wilson, Desmond, *Undermining Peace*, Belfast 1992.

Wituliet, Theo, *A Place in the Sun*, SCM Press Ltd, London 1985.

Other Publications

Aisling magazine, Quarterly, Aran Islands.

A Question of Choices, Submission to the Dáil and Seanad on Aspects of the 1992 Budget from the Justice Commission of the CMRS, 1992.

Being a Priest in Ireland Today, AGM of NCPI, Dominican Publications, Dublin 1988.

Civil Liberties in Northern Ireland – The CAJ Handbook, Committee of the Administration of Justice, Belfast 1990.

Directory of Discrimination, The Equality Working Group, Belfast 1991.

Gaudium et Spes, CTS, London 1966.

Good News in a Divided Society – Papers of the 1991 AGM of the National Conference of Priests of Ireland, Dominican Publications, Dublin 1992.

Growing Exclusion, CMRS Submission for 1993 Budget, The Justice Commission, CMRS, Milltown, Dublin 1993.

Unemployment, Jobs and the 1990s, Council for Social Welfare, Dublin 1989.

Unemployment in West Belfast, The Obair Report, compiled by Bill Rolston and Mike Tomlinson with Geraldine McAteer, Beyond the Pale Publications 1988.

Work is the Key, Veritas, Dublin 1992.

Work of Justice, The, Bishops Pastoral, Veritas, Dublin 1977.